# NOMO

## THE
## INSIDE STORY
## ON
## BASEBALL'S HOTTEST
## SENSATION

---

## Herb Fagen

A SIGNET BOOK

SIGNET
Published by the Penguin Group
Penguin Books USA Inc., 375 Hudson Street,
New York, New York 10014, U.S.A.
Penguin Books Ltd, 27 Wrights Lane,
London W8 5TZ, England
Penguin Books Australia Ltd, Ringwood,
Victoria, Australia
Penguin Books Canada Ltd, 10 Alcorn Avenue,
Toronto, Ontario, Canada M4V 3B2
Penguin Books (N.Z.) Ltd, 182–190 Wairau Road,
Auckland 10, New Zealand

Penguin Books Ltd, Registered Offices:
Harmondsworth, Middlesex, England

First published by Signet, an imprint of Dutton Signet,
a division of Penguin Books USA Inc.

First Printing, April, 1996
10  9  8  7  6  5  4  3  2  1

Printed in the United States of America

**IN A STYLE REMINISCENT OF FORMER
DODGER FERNANDO VALENZUELA,
BASEBALL'S LATEST ROOKIE SENSATION
CONFOUNDS BATTERS AND DELIGHTS
FANS EVERYWHERE.**

But just how good a pitcher is Hideo Nomo? Well,
his stats indicate that he's very, very good. In his first
major league season he was named Rookie of the
Year, was voted National League Pitcher-of-the-
Month for June, carried a 6–1 record and a 1.99
earned run average into the first week of July, led the
National League with 119 strikeouts as of July 6, set a
Dodger rookie record with 16 strikeouts against the
Pirates on June 14, and amassed a four-game strikeout total of 50, breaking Dodger legend and Hall-of-
Famer Sandy Koufax's team record of 49, set back in
1965. And in his historic start at the All-Star Game,
he gave up just one hit in two brilliant innings, and
struck out three batters, including American League
stars Albert Belle and Edgar Martinez.

# N O M O

**Herb Fagen** is a regular contributor to *Baseball Digest* and
*USA Today/Baseball Weekly* and the co-author, with Minnie
Minoso, of *Just Call Me Minnie: My Six Decades in Baseball*.
He lives in Walnut Creek, California.

*To My Mom*

# CONTENTS

# Contents

# ACKNOWLEDGMENTS

Any list of acknowledgments must start with my agent, Jake Elwell of Wieser & Wieser, who from the start—before the mega strikeouts and the rampant Nomomania—had the foresight to think that there could be a good story here. And to Deb Brody, Senior Editor at Dutton-Signet, for her editorial expertise. My deep thanks to both the Los Angeles Dodgers and the San Francisco Giants for extending me press credentials.

My appreciation to the major league players who helped me along with a comment or two, especially Matt Williams, Tony Gwynn, Royce Clayton, Marvin Bernard, Ken Caminiti, Mike Piazza, and Todd Worrell. Thanks also to San Francisco Giants manager Dusty Baker, and coaches Wendell Kim of the Giants and Graig Nettles of the San Diego Padres.

The following old-time stars provided loads of insight from a different era: Ferris Fain, Claude Passeau, Andy Pafko, Minnie Minoso, Orlando Cepeda, Chico Carrasquel, and Larry Jansen.

To those in the Japanese-American community who gave so generously of their time and energy, I owe a great deal of thanks and appreciation:

# Acknowledgments

Akira Matsuo, president and publisher of the *Hokubei Mainichi*, and photographer Nobuyuki Aoyagi for permission to use their excellent photographs. Mitsufumi Okabe, president of Japan Television Network, Takeo Babe Utsumi, writer and baseball expert. Karen Kinoshita, director of catering at the Miyako Hotel and a great baseball fan. And Steve Nakajo, who was my liaison to the Japanese-American Community here in northern California.

Thanks too to Tony Woods, purchasing director at the Miyako Hotel in San Francisco and former big league ballplayer, for lending his insight, both personal and professional. To Jonah Phillips, my research assistant, and Sally Landis, who proofed the chapters, thanks so much.

I have been following baseball a long time. My first awareness of the game came when I was five. My father got up early one morning. I asked him where he was going. He said he was going to the ballpark. It was the last game of the World Series. The year was 1945, and the Cubs were playing the Tigers in the series that year. We watched a lot of baseball together over the next 48 years. He loved his Cubs, but never got to see them in a World Series again. Whenever I sit down to write a baseball story or baseball book, I think of him. I know he would have loved to have seen Nomo pitch.

If you can talk with crowds and keep your virtue
   or walk with kings—nor lose the common touch,
If neither foes nor loving friends can hurt you,
   If all men count with you, but none too much;
      If you can fill the unforgiving minute,
      with sixty seconds worth of distance run,
Yours is the earth and everything that's in it,
   and—which is more—you'll be a Man, my son!

—RUDYARD KIPLING

# INTRODUCTION

On November 8, 1995, Japanese-born pitcher Hideo Nomo was chosen National League Rookie of the Year by the Baseball Writers of America. It was a deserving award for a deserving athlete. The award also put Nomo in some select company. Since its inception in 1947, such Hall of Famers as Jackie Robinson, Willie Mays, Willie McCovey, Billy Williams, Tom Seaver, and Johnny Bench have been chosen as the National League's top rookie. So have Orlando Cepeda, Dick Allen, Andre Dawson, and Pete Rose.

The story of Hideo Nomo captured the fancy of the entire baseball world in 1995. Moreover, it could not have happened at a better time. Baseball fans throughout the country were soured by an eight-month strike, a canceled World Series, and an uncertain season opener. Nomo gave the game a new joy, a new excitement. His "tornado-like" delivery fascinated fans and players alike. His fastball could exceed 90 mph, and his forkball, some old timers say, is among the best they have ever seen.

But the true essence of Hideo Nomo far transcends the marvelous numbers he put on the board, and some were extraordinary indeed. The 1995 baseball season, as bereft as it was to some, was full of outstanding numbers: Cleveland Indian Albert Belle's 50 home runs and 50 doubles, Atlanta Braves pitcher Greg Maddux's 19–2 record, third straight ERA under 2.00, and a fourth straight Cy Young Award. Eddie Murray joined the exclusive 3,000 hit club in 1995, and Cal Ripken, Jr., broke Lou Gehrig's "unbreakable" Iron Man record of 2,130 consecutive games. The Cleveland Indians won 100 ball games and their first American League pennant since 1954. The Braves won the first world championship of any sort for the city of Atlanta. And Tony Gwynn won his sixth National League batting title.

What makes Hideo Nomo's story different from the rest is its human quality. It goes beyond baseball, beyond media hype, beyond the norm. Because Nomo's story is the story of a journey, it is an odyssey in the truest sense of the term.

It's a story of a man chasing a dream, far beyond his homeland, to a faraway shore of which he knew very little. He was a star, a celebrity at home in Japan, who simply wanted to play baseball against the best in the world. Moreover, it is a story that doesn't end with the final page of this book. As Winston Churchill once said: it's not the end, but rather "it's the end of the beginning."

# NOMO

# 1

# July 11, 1995

The temperature hovered over the hundred-degree mark in Arlington, Texas, the night of July 11, 1995. It was the site of the 66th All-Star Game. The Texas Rangers' $195 million baseball stadium is a gorgeous facility. Little expense was spared to make this year's mid-summer classic a gala affair.

All-time pitching greats Nolan Ryan and Ferguson Jenkins, both of whom toiled long, hard innings for the Rangers in the past, were honorary team captains. Ryan played 27 big-league seasons and is baseball's all-time strikeout king, while Jenkins, the pitching coach of the Chicago Cubs, is the only major league hurler to strike out more than 3,000 and walk fewer than 1,000 batters over a 19-year Hall of Fame career.

17

A crowd of more than 50,000 packed the park to capacity. Media by the hundreds gathered to report and chronicle the game. There were many old-timers as well. Fifty-nine-year-old Harmon Killebrew, who belted a Hall of Fame total 573 home runs, second in the American League only to Babe Ruth, was there. So were Larry Doby, the American League's first black major leaguer, and Orlando Cepeda, baseball's "Baby Bull," who is the only major leaguer unanimously chosen both Rookie of the Year (1958) and MVP (1967). They and other past baseball greats were warming up for the old-timers "Legends of the Game All-Star Classic," a crowd-pleasing prelude to the big game itself.

Gaylord Perry, far wider and grayer than during his playing days, and a Hall of Fame career that garnered him 314 wins and a Cy Young Award in each league, trotted across the field with his three-year-old grandson on his shoulder. He then posed for a picture with pitcher Masanori Murakami, who thirty years ago was the first Japanese-born player to play big league baseball. The whole ensemble was a living reminder of what baseball once was.

Due to the baseball strike and lingering fan disenchantment and apathy, early interest in the game paled by comparison with other years. A good indicator was a 1995 All-Star vote numbering just under six million, which was less than Ken Griffey, Jr.'s 1994 vote total alone, when more than 14 million ballots were punched. Yet by game time the 1995 mid-summer classic had created an interest and anticipation well beyond most All-Star contests.

Waiting in the wings to start the 66th All-Star Game for Manager Felipe Alou's National League All-Stars was Japanese right-hander Hideo Nomo of the Los Angeles Dodgers. Called "The Tornado" by the baseball world because of his unorthodox pitching motion, Nomo was major league baseball's reigning poster boy. As Pete Williams aptly wrote in his cover report for *Baseball Weekly*, "With the exception of a certain basketball star who tried to reach the major leagues recently, no player has attracted the publicity of Nomo." The reference was clear. Last year Michael Jordan was the talk of baseball. This year it was Hideo Nomo. But with one big difference. Nomo had enormous baseball talent.

Not only had Nomo almost single-handedly rejuvenated the depleted baseball scene here in the U.S., but in Tokyo and other Japanese cities people were gathering on the street to watch the 26-year-old right-hander with his trademark delivery on giant television screens.

"He reminds me of Ewell 'The Whip' Blackwell from our era," said Andy Pafko, one of the many former stars invited to join the All-Star festivities and who played in four All-Star games and four World Series during the 1940s and '50s. "As with Blackwell, who gave our guys such fits back then, Nomo hides the ball so well that hitters just can't seem to pick up on it."

By assuming starting honors for the National League All-Stars, Nomo became only the fourth rookie pitcher from either league, and the first since Fernando Valenzuela in 1981, to start an All-Star Game. He was also the star of two Nike ads that debuted during the game, each opening with a scene of a tornado in slow motion. His souvenir jackets sold for $150 at Dodger Stadium. He spoke no English, but that didn't matter. "His fastball and forkball beat any language barrier," said an admiring Tony Gwynn shortly before the game. "He's the most dominant rookie to come into the game since I've been around," National League MVP candidate Ron Gant was quick to attest. Similarly, when asked whom he could compare Nomo to, San Francisco slugger Matt Williams replied instantly, "Nobody. That's who I compare him to."

"Dodger Nomo One of a Kind: Japanese Rookie Pitcher Takes 'Nomomania' to Texas," Joan Ryan wrote in the *San Francisco Chronicle*. Nomo had become so big, in fact, that he had two conferences the day before: one during the morning for the two starting pitchers, Nomo and Seattle's Randy Johnson, then another after practice in the afternoon. "I'm looking forward to seeing Nomo pitch," Johnson stated. "He's the equivalent of Michael Jordan in Japan."

Texas Governor George Bush, Jr., held his own news conference at the ballpark, where he pitched Nomo to the press. "He's great for the game. It's one of the best things to happen to baseball in a long time."

Because Nomo speaks almost no English, his interviews and press conferences are conducted through an interpreter. In fact, Nomo was the first player to have a full-time interpreter with him at all times. Dressed in a gray suit for the morning press conference, he spoke in the soft voice of a child. He said that being chosen for the game was an honor, beyond all his expectations for the year. This was his greatest thrill, he insisted, more than anything he had achieved in Japan. After the press conference he walked onto the field with the rest of the National League All-Stars. The entourage of cameramen and reporters escorting him was so great that security was summoned to herd the media away and allow Nomo to get on with his necessary work.

Just how good a pitcher was Hideo Nomo at the All-Star break? He was good enough to carry a 6–1 record and a 1.99 earned run average into the first week of July. He led the National League with 119 strikeouts on July 6, and set a Dodger rookie record with 16 strikeouts against the Pittsburgh Pirates on June 16. He amassed a four-game total of 50 strikeouts, breaking Sandy Koufax's team record of 39 set in 1965. He was voted the National League pitcher for the month for June, putting together a fabulous 6–0 record and 0.89 ERA. He allowed just 4.89 base hits per nine innings—almost two hits less than three-time Cy Young winner Greg Maddux.

Moreover, at the All-Star break the celebrated Japanese rookie was on a record-setting pace. Nomo's strikeout rate of 11.62 per nine innings pitched topped Nolan Ryan's 1987 National League rate of 11.48 for the Houston Astros. Only his All-

Star opponent Randy Johnson's 1995 rate of 12.99 had ever been better.

Since its inception in 1933 by *Chicago Tribune* sportswriter Arch Ward, the All-Star Game has become a baseball institution. The city of Chicago was hosting the Century of Progress Exposition in 1933, a worthy diversion to the breadlines and unemployment of the Great Depression. To enhance the festivities Arch Ward conceived the idea of a one-time exhibition game featuring the game's greatest players, with the fans voting for their favorite players.

But the All-Star Game was not to be the one-time baseball exhibition Arch Ward had intended. Rather it became a true staple of our national pastime—and with the exception of 1945, when wartime travel restrictions prevented its play—it has remained so throughout the years. A wonderful and exciting mid-season contest, the All-Star Game has provided thrills, excitement, and special moments that remain forever imprinted into the lore and legacy of the grand old game.

It's been more than sixty years since that landmark contest on July 6, 1933, at Comiskey Park, Chicago, when baseball legends John McGraw and Connie Mack first managed their respective National and American League squads. Appropriately it was Babe Ruth, the "Sultan of Swat" himself, who at age 38 electrified the fans by hitting the first All-Star game home run, a two-run shot in the third inning, paving the way for a 4–2 American League win.

In 1995 all eyes were on Hideo Nomo, who only four months earlier had not even been sure he would make the Dodger squad. Pre-game hype prevailed as rarely before, and Nomo was as good as advertised. Everything was in place as he delivered his first pitch to Cleveland Indian Kenny Lofton: that high kick, the wild arm movements, the severely arched back turning ominously away from the batter.

The feisty Lofton, hitting .315 with five home runs and 27 RBIs on the year, lined a foul ball to right field before striking out on two Nomo fastballs. The Indians' outstanding second baseman Carlos Baerga was next. He singled to right field but was promptly thrown out stealing—the only American league batter to reach base off Nomo. Seattle's Edgar Martinez, whose .363 average topped all American League hitters, then became Nomo's second strikeout victim as he fanned to end the inning.

Nomo set the American League down with even

quicker dispatch in the second inning. White Sox slugger Frank Thomas, baseball's "Big Hurt" and two-time American League MVP, lifted a mile-high pop up behind the plate that catcher Mike Piazza put away. Next came Cleveland's hard-hitting Albert Belle. With two strikes on him, he was appropriately looking for a forkball. Instead he let a Nomo fastball slip by him for a called third strike, becoming Nomo's third strikeout victim. Nomo then retired the side in order when the Orioles' Cal Ripken, Jr., lined a shot to right that Tony Gwynn speared with a running catch.

Nomo's All-Star work was done, and he did it splendidly. He had pitched to six of the American League's toughest batters. He allowed one hit, struck out three, and walked none. Among those who were impressed thoroughly was eighty-seven-year-old Claude Passeau, who surrendered Ted Williams's infamous 1941 all-star shot more than fifty years ago.

"I like this young fellow Nomo, said Passeau, who watched the game from his home in Lucedale, Mississippi. "His delivery is deceptive and he has good stuff. But what I really like about him is the way he pitches. He's smart. He uses his head like that Maddux fellow."

It had been a storybook tale pure and simple, an

unfolding baseball drama so perfectly crafted, so deftly scripted. It couldn't have come at a better time either. Major league baseball was in a depressed state. Attendance had dropped to a recent record low, down by 20 percent from the previous year. Baseball was in trouble, big trouble, many sages argued. Disenchanted by the new breed of millionaires in pinstripes, and an eight-month baseball strike, fans were staying home and the networks were losing markets.

Most refreshing, however, was that when people talked about Nomo, they talked deliveries and not dollars. "Baseball needs him," said 1981 Cy Young winner Fernando Valenzuela, who like Nomo set the baseball world on its heels his rookie season. "In my rookie year of 1981 we had a strike, and what I did was important for baseball. Now that we had another strike, we need somebody else to come through. Maybe he can get people to come to the park again. That would be nice!"

Not only Nomo's pitching credits glittered; his memorabilia had also become pure gold. "Nomo Mania" had entered the lexicon of the prevailing baseball lingo. "Nomo is already a bigger sell than Fernando Valenzuela ever was," commented Scott Evers, who has manned a souvenir stand at Dodger Stadium for many years. "I didn't expect it to be this big," he told the *Los Angeles Times*. "We can't keep enough merchandise in my stands. Usually people come by here and buy one or two dollars in knickknacks. People are buying two or three Nomo shirts at a time. It's great!"

Yet behind the fastballs and forkballs, behind the strange delivery and the mega strikeouts, behind the tornado hype and the rampant Nomo Mania sweeping two countries, is a much larger story. It is an uplifting tale of courage and grit, of dreams believed and of dreams followed. It is a rare story that crosses continents and cultures, a story that provides a much needed bridge between East and West.

Nomo's story is history and drama. It is America and it is Japan, two countries united under a common umbrella called baseball. The story of Hideo Nomo is of the here and now. But its antecedents are of a different era, a different time, a different world. And it's to this world that we must first turn.

# 2

# "You Gotta Have Wa," Mr. O'Doul

**F**ifty years ago, when American and Japanese forces were locked in fierce wartime combat, Japanese soldiers responded to the taunts of American GIs by shouting back invectives like "To hell with Babe Ruth! To hell with Joe DiMaggio!" Many an ex-serviceman has attested to such slurs, although the four-letter words, they insist, were far nastier.

There are other verifiable wartime anecdotes as well. On one Pacific island a dead Japanese soldier named Hikichi Kazuo was identified by newspaper clippings as a star third baseman for Osaka of Japan's major league. The war also gave one minor league player the hope of settling an old score. Upon enlisting in the navy, Fred Collins, who played for Kansas City in the American Associa-

tion, said he wanted to find an individual whom
he encountered years before while pitching against
a touring Japanese team. "I would have had a
shutout if this little guy hadn't hit me for two
home runs," Collins said. "I just want to get my
hands on him."

Babe Ruth actually played baseball in Japan. So
did Joe DiMaggio, the Yankee Clipper. For years
the Japanese had been enamored with our national
pastime. In fact, ten years before Pearl Harbor, the
great Lefty O'Doul brought a team of American
all-stars to play baseball in Japan. O'Doul was
one of the premier ballplayers of his or any other
baseball generation. He was so good that only Ty
Cobb, Rogers Hornsby, and Shoeless Joe Jackson
hold a higher lifetime average.

O'Doul was an enormous student of the game,
and his contributions to the growth and development of baseball in Japan is so great that he re-
mains as well known in Japanese circles as he is
among American baseball pundits and historians.
Because of all this, sportswriters in his home town
of San Francisco dubbed O'Doul, the "Father of
Baseball in Japan."

Takio "Babe" Utsumi was born in Stockton, California, more than 70 years ago, and has been
involved with baseball all his life. He well remem-

bers O'Doul's involvement with the Japanese community, here and abroad.

"People out here really liked Lefty O'Doul. He was a San Franciscan from an area we called 'Butcher Town.' To me he's a beloved figure, and we've always associated him with San Francisco Bay. He was great for baseball in Japan, and was one of the first guys to go down there. He was a flamboyant guy and a hell of a hitter too. Somehow they never got around to putting him in the Hall of Fame."

In 1931 O'Doul brought an all-star team consisting of future Hall of Famers Lou Gehrig, Lefty Grove, Mickey Cochrane, Frankie Frisch, Rabbit Maranville, George Kelly, and Al Simmons to Japan on a baseball tour. After a two-week Pacific crossing on a Japanese luxury liner, the American all-stars played seventeen games against university teams, commercial teams, and a Japanese all-star team, sweeping all seventeen.

Played before capacity crowds that ran as high as 75,000 in some stadiums, the tour was a rousing success. The only blight came in the seventh game when Lou Gehrig was hit by a pitch during a 2–0 win over Keio University, suffered two broken bones in his right hand, and was unable to play for the remainder of the trip. Who could imagine that these would be the only games Gehrig would miss to injury in 15 years, while playing a record 2,130 consecutive games for the New York Yankees?

But the real plum was as yet missing from O'Doul's squad of all-stars. Japanese fans, like all others, wanted to see the Babe. But Ruth was reportedly busy making a movie in California at the time. It was not easy for O'Doul to land the coveted "Sultan of Swat." In fact, it took three years before O'Doul was able to coax his old pal from the Yankee days to join his all-stars. Finally with some added persuasion from Mrs. Ruth, the Bambino agreed to join the squad in 1934.

It was the stuff from which movies are made, only this scenario was entirely real. The Japanese loved the Babe, and the Babe loved his reception. When the American team paraded in open cars down the Ginza in Tokyo, the Babe's car was in the front of the pack. Adoring fans crowded so tightly around his car that the whole cavalcade was forced to a dead halt. According to some newspaper accounts, more than a million people came out to see Babe Ruth.

"It seemed like all Tokyo was out, waving and yelling," the late Charlie Gehringer told author Donald Honig many years later. "We could hardly get our cars through, the streets were so jammed.

What was interesting was that they knew who we all were. You'd think being so many miles away and of such a different culture, the whole thing would have been so strange to them. But apparently they had been following big league baseball for years, and gee, they knew us all. Especially Ruth, of course. They made a terrific fuss over him, and he loved it."

Of course he did, and why not? The Americans had played before large crowds before, but never as many as the 100,000 who pushed their way into Meji Stadium in Tokyo. Natural showman that he was, Ruth took advantage of a torrential rain storm. When a fan came out of the stands in the first inning and handed over his umbrella, Ruth and the fan exchanged courteous bows. To show his appreciation, the Babe played the entire game, except when he was batting, under the umbrella.

Two years earlier, when O'Doul had come to Japan, in 1932 he brought Washington Senator catcher Moe Berg, and Chicago White Sox pitcher Ted Lyons along to coach Big Six University League players in Tokyo. Like O'Doul, Moe Berg quickly fell in love with Japan. At least that's how it seemed. He even learned to speak Japanese. Years later it was revealed that Berg secretly took photos of Tokyo from the roof of St. Luke's International, which later were used to help plan U.S. bombing raids during World War II.

Yet for Lefty O'Doul, baseball in Japan was more than just crowded stadiums and cheering crowds. During all of his visits during the 1930s, then after the war years into the 1950s, he concentrated on teaching as well. He found the Japanese to be receptive pupils.

"I like the people," he told an interviewer. "See, I like people who you're not wasting your time on, trying to help them. American kids know more than the coach. Teaching Japanese and Americans is like night and day." His impact on Japanese baseball was so great, and baseball became so popular in Japan during the 1930s, that it almost survived without interruption during World War II—despite being the invention and national pastime of the enemy. Not until October 1944 was play suspended. To show the priority of baseball in wartime Japan, consider that some 10,000 geisha houses and other amusement centers were shut down a year earlier.

Baseball in Japan actually goes back to the nineteenth century. To understand the true essence of Hideo Nomo's story, we should at least take a brief look at the history and development of Japanese baseball.

The story of baseball in Japan and its indigenous roots is fascinating. And nowhere is it dealt with better than in two fine books by Robert Whiting, *You Gotta Have Wa* (1990) and *The Chrysanthemum and the Bat* (1977).

Japanese baseball has assumed a life of its own, and even though Americans and Japanese play by almost the same rules, the two philosophies are quite different. On a Japanese ball club, *wa*—the perfect harmony of team unity—always comes first. So in some ways, it can be said that Nomo's thrust toward American baseball may well show an independence and spirit more akin to American players than his Japanese counterparts.

Many folks are surprised to learn that baseball was first introduced to Japan in 1873, when a Christian missionary named Horace Wilson taught the game to university students in Tokyo. The first game between a Japanese and an American team was played as early as 1896, when a Tokyo school nine challenged the American Athletic Club of Yokohama.

According to Robert Whiting, a ragtag American team made up of merchants, traders, and missionaries living in Yokohama was repeatedly trounced by a Japanese preparatory school team that trained so extensively that its players were said to urinate blood at the end of a practice.

The school's pitcher, Katoro Mariyama, became such a celebrity that he spawned a popular saying: "To be hit by Moriyama's fastball is an honor exceeded only by being crushed under the wheels of the imperial carriage."

In 1905 a Waseda University team made a trip to California to play a series of games against American college teams. The New York Giants and the Chicago White Sox played three games in Japan during their round-the-world tour in 1913. During the 1920s American All-Star and Negro League teams played in Japan on a regular basis. By 1930 baseball had become so popular in Japan that it rivaled sumo wrestling as a national pastime.

Baseball had been ingrained into the Japanese culture to such a great extent that it became one of the major staples of Japanese Americans who languished in the internment camps during World War II. From the second decade of the twentieth century, baseball was the most popular sport in the Japanese-American community. Given the prewar popularity of baseball, its prominence in the wartime camps is hardly surprising. And while there was competition in many sports, including basketball, football, boxing, and softball, none was pursued with the passion devoted to baseball.

"Babe" Utsumi recalls those difficult days, both before and during the war. Growing up in Stockton, he lived primarily in a Japanese ghetto. He was a *nisei* (a second-generation Japanese American), and the first of his family to be born in the United States. The kids loved playing baseball, and it became even more special to Babe because his father was so involved. In northern California towns like Stockton, Alameda, San Jose, and Sacramento, parks and stadiums sprang up wherever there was a Japanese community. "We sponsored these teams, and they were red-hot," Utsumi says.

It's no sidebar in our history that the 442nd Regiment of Japanese Americans became the most highly decorated outfit of World War II. Even after fifty years, many Japanese Americans still point to baseball as one of the few bright spots of a dark time. "I think baseball was the main salvation against the loneliness of the camps," said Bill Motsumoto. "More than anything, it got people together. If it hadn't been for baseball, it would have been unbearable."

Lefty O'Doul helped breach the chasm created by World War II. As manager of the San Francisco

Seals in the Pacific Coast League, he arrived in Japan in 1949 to find the Japanese starving for baseball. General Douglas MacArthur, commanding the U.S. occupation, encouraged the rebirth of the game, and ordered the clearing of the Yomiuri Giants stadium, which had been converted into an ammunition dump. O'Doul was up to the task. The San Francisco Seals gave dozens of clinics and played ten games in Japan, four against American service teams, six against Japanese clubs. The visit raised more than $100,000 for Japanese charities.

In forty days O'Doul and his group of minor league ballplayers from the States helped restore the nation's pride, and eased much of the postwar tension in American and Japanese relations. "All the diplomats put together would not have been able to do that. This is the greatest piece of diplomacy ever," said an admiring General MacArthur. Emperor Hirohito was so grateful that he summoned Lefty O'Doul, Seals president Paul Fagan, and vice-president Charlie Graham to thank them personally for all they had done for his country.

Lefty O'Doul's influence on baseball in Japan did not end there. He and Joe DiMaggio traveled together several times during the 1950s to coach Japanese players. In 1951 O'Doul took his first postwar team of big leaguers to Japan to play sixteen games against Japanese all star-teams from the Central and Pacific leagues.

Appropriately called "O'Doul's All-Stars," the team included Joe and Dom DiMaggio, New York Yankee rookie second baseman Billy Martin, pitchers Eddie Lopat of the Yankees, Mel Parnell of the Red Sox, Bobby Shantz of the Philadelphia Athletics, and American League batting champion, Ferris Fain. He had been on O'Doul's 1946 San Francisco Seals squad that took the Pacific Coast League title with a record of 115–68.

"Lefty was a father figure to me. I learned a lot from him. He could really teach," says Fain. "Just a great teacher and a great manager. He was the best I ever played for. When he asked me to be a part of his first postwar squad to go to Japan, I was really thrilled and honored."

Fain, who would capture his second straight American League batting title for the Philadelphia Athletics in 1952, fondly recalls that visit as a member of O'Doul's All-Stars.

"What a wonderful experience," says the 74-year-old Fain from his Georgetown, California, home. "The Japanese loved their baseball and were among the warmest and most honest people I have known. They were also great competitors. We played sixteen games against various Japanese all-star teams. They played us hard and sometimes close. They almost beat us one game, but Joe [DiMaggio] hit one out of the park in the dark. The ball might still be going, it was hit so hard. It tied it up for us, and then the game was called on account of darkness. Of course, Joe was the feature attraction in Japan just as he was back home. He had that marvelous and dignified persona, and people seemed to worship him wherever we went."

During his earliest postwar visits O'Doul began to sell the Japanese on the idea that the level of their play would improve significantly if they developed farm teams. This finally came to fruition in 1954, when the first Japanese minor league was formed. His influence on Japanese baseball had become so far-reaching that he even determined what uniforms players should wear. To this day the Yomiuri Giants wear uniforms nearly identical to that worn by O'Doul when he played for the New York Giants in 1933–34. The name Giants in the same black and orange lettering emblazon their shirts.

When Lefty O'Doul died of a heart attack in San Francisco in 1969—ironically on December 7— Pearl Harbor Day—Japanese consul Seichi Shima led a delegation of his country to the funeral. "No single man did more to reestablish faith and friendship between our two nations than did Lefty O'Doul," said Monsignor Vincent Breen, directing his eulogy at Japanese and American alike.

In a column published shortly after O'Doul's death, Pulitzer-Prize winning sports columnist Red Smith recalled another incident in O'Doul's long and warm relationship with the Japanese:

"In a Catholic mission in Tokyo, the kids were preparing for confirmation. They were told they had the privilege of adding a new name to that received at baptism, but little Toshi couldn't think of a saint's name he would like to adopt.

" 'Why don't you choose Francis? suggested the nun who was his teacher—for St. Francis de Sales.

" 'Ah, so,' Toshi said.

"A few days later, the bishop was about to administer the sacrament.

" 'And what's your confirmation name?' he was asked.

"Toshi's face lit up.

" 'San Francisco Seals,' he said."

Lefty O'Doul died in 1969, the year the New York Mets became the baseball champions of the world. One year earlier, on August 31, 1968, Hideo Nomo was born in Osaka, Japan.

# 3

# "Mashi," Sadahara, and Young Hideo

In 1968, the United States was in a state of political and social chaos. The Vietnam War had torn the social fabric asunder, reaching its apex by 1968.

To many Americans it appeared that the country was being torn apart at the seams. On January 31, 1968, Americans saw a vastly different kind of war. In the so-called Tet Offensive, thousands of Communist soldiers launched a surprise attack against South Vietnam's supposedly impregnable urban areas. Two months later, a haggard Lyndon Johnson stunned an entire nation by announcing he would neither seek nor accept his party's nomination for another term as president.

Then on April 4th the nation mourned the assassination of Martin Luther King, Jr. Urban ghettoes soon erupted in uncontrolled violence. In early June, moments after being declared winner of the California primary, Robert Kennedy was shot to death. By late August, TV cameras captured the violence taking place between the police and anti-war protesters at the Democratic National Convention in Chicago. In November a tired nation elected Richard M. Nixon as its thirty-seventh president.

In the world of baseball, the Detroit Tigers defeated the St. Louis Cardinals in seven games to become world champs. The Red Sox's Carl Yastrzemski won the American League batting title with a .301 average, the lowest in major league history. Pete Rose hit .335 for the Cincinnati Reds to become the first switch hitter in National League history to lead the league in hitting.

Detroit's Denny McLain won 31 games to become the first 30-game winner since 1934. The Cardinals' Bob Gibson threw 13 shutouts and posted a 1.12 ERA, lowest since 1914. McLain and Gibson won both the Cy Young and MVP awards in their respective leagues.

Don Drysdale of the Dodgers pitched 58 consecutive scoreless innings for a major league record. The Giants' Juan Marichal won 26 games and paced the National League with 30 complete games. He became the only three-time 25-game winner, and only six-time 20-game winner never to win a Cy Young Award. Catfish Hunter of the Oakland A's pitched a perfect game against the Twins, and the Cleveland Indians' Luis Tiant, who led the American League with a 1.60 ERA, struck out 19 batters in a ten-inning game.

Four teams scored fewer than 500 runs in 1968. The A's moved from Kansas City to Oakland and topped the American League with a .240 BA, lowest in major league history. The once mighty New York Yankees set a record for lowest team batting average, hitting just .214. Little wonder that in the United States, 1968 was called the "Year of the Pitcher."

In Osaka, Japan, where Hideo Nomo was born on August 31, 1968, life was more stable, at least in the political and social realm. Japan had survived the postwar occupation intact. Douglas MacArthur became a hero, the warlords were history, and the emperor still reigned. The new Japanese constitution renounced war forever and always. Instead the Japanese began to focus their considerable skills toward business, manufacturing, and industry. The GNP was steadily rising, and the nation was on an economic surge.

Like many kids in the United States, Hideo Nomo grew up loving baseball. He spent long hours playing it in the parks and sandlots of Osaka, just as kids all over America did. From his youngest years he yearned to play professional baseball. "My parents were always big baseball fans, and I wanted to be a professional baseball player ever since I was in elementary school," Nomo told twelve-year-old Deana Vasquez of Chino Hills, California, in an interview arranged by MLB for Kids.

But Nomo did not start out as pitcher. He was an outfielder who turned to pitching in junior high school because, in his own words, "I wasn't a very good hitter." No one taught him the tornado-like motion that later garnered him his fame. "I just made it up myself, and it worked for me."

Third-base coach Wendell Kim of the San Francisco Giants says there are pitchers in the Far East who throw somewhat like Nomo but not exactly. "In Korea and even in Japan there is some similarity. There the pitching deliveries are different from those in the United States, much more sidearm and almost underarm."

Ken Caminiti, the San Diego Padres' hard-hitting third baseman, concurs. He recalls playing against South Korea and Japan in the 1984 Olympics. "When I was on the Olympic team I think we played the South Koreans and the Japanese about thirteen times. Almost all of their pitchers were sidearmers, herky-jerky types. But I've never seen a delivery like Nomo's, never! It's hard to pick up the ball."

Akira Matsuo is president and publisher of the Mainichi Newspapers, a daily newspaper with a circulation of over 10,000 subscribers in northern California. Born and raised in Japan, Matsuo came to the United States almost 20 years ago. A trim and athletic man in his early fifties, Matsuo grew up playing baseball in his native country. He too followed the prescribed route for Japanese youngsters in love with the game. Unlike Nomo, however, he didn't take his talent into the professional arena. Yes, there are many sidearm pitchers in Japan, he contends, but none at all like Nomo. "He is a very unique pitcher," Matsuo states. "Nomo's delivery is unique there as it is here."

Matsuo is quick to note that baseball is different in Japan. The strategy is more precise, the training more arduous, and the methods more traditional. Because there are only 12 professional teams, and just one minor league there are fewer players in Japan compared to the United States. So the baseball community is rather small and intimate.

Hideo Nomo is responsible for allowing more Japanese to become interested in American baseball, Matsuo contends. But there was always a fascination with American baseball and its players. As a teenager Matsuo remembers seeing the New York Yankees play baseball in Japan. "When I was growing up and playing baseball, I knew all about Mickey Mantle and Yogi Berra. Everyone seemed to know about the New York Yankees because they were to the United States what the Tokyo Giants were to us here in Japan."

The main reasons why Nomo was able to establish himself in Japan at an early age was because of the importance of high school baseball. Unlike America, where football and basketball are the marquee prep sports, in Japan high school baseball is bigger than all other sports combined.

The National High School Tournament is one of the year's biggest events. It is televised over the entire country, so a high school baseball star in Japan can easily capture the fancy of an entire nation. So strong is high school baseball that it is even more popular than college baseball.

"High school baseball in Japan is equivalent to basketball in the United States," says Takeo "Babe" Utsumi, a retired baker who today writes a column for the *Hokubei Mainichi*. "It is not unusual to have 15,000 people for a high school tournament in Japan. When you have a tournament in Osaka, you can draw 50,000. You just can't believe it. Another thing about Japan is if you play baseball, that's all you play. Not basketball or football. You just play baseball and train all year long."

Baseball players train much harder in Japan. And it's a regimen of training that many Americans who later played there have found difficult. Notes Utsumi, "In America they hate all that running. Run, run, run, and a lot of Americans don't like that. People don't seem to realize that Sadaharo Oh trained himself like a samurai."

Japanese baseball stars rarely go right to the professional ranks. Nor even on to college immediately. The next step following high school is something called company ball, which is similar to the old factory or industrial teams here in the U.S. In Latin countries such as Cuba, these teams were the testing grounds for such future big league stars as the legendary Minnie Minoso, who went from the sugarcane fields of Cuba to stardom with the Chicago White Sox in the 1950s, and is baseball's only six-decade player.

Following graduation from Seijo High School in Osaka, Nomo began playing for a company team. It was only after seeing how hard he could throw a baseball, and what his baffling forkball could do, that the Kinetsu Buffaloes of Japan's Pacific League signed him to a professional contract.

But the Buffaloes never had the popularity of a team like the Tokyo Giants. Nor did the Pacific League enjoy the fanfare of the Central League. So when Nomo joined the Buffaloes, not as many people were watching him as there might have been had he played for a higher-profile club.

A natural question arises: with baseball so popular in Japan, why has it taken so long for a Japanese player to make it to the American major leagues? The color line for blacks crumbled in 1947, when Jackie Robinson and Larry Doby became the first blacks to integrate the National and American leagues. By the early 1950s Latin players like Chico Carrasquel and Minnie Minoso were already genuine all-stars. With the rich baseball tradition in Japan, what has held Japanese players back?

The reasons are many and varied, and will be examined more closely later. But for now it should be made clear that Hideo Nomo was not the first Japanese to play major league baseball in the United States. That honor belongs to Masanori Murakami. And any story on Nomo would be incomplete without touching on "Mashi" Murakami. In 1964-65, this left-handed pitcher became the first player from Japan to reach the major leagues.

Still well remembered among the Japanese community in the Bay Area, Murakami was recently honored by the Giants. He is a radio commentator in Japan today, and an icon in his own right, and the Giants enlisted his services when they tried to sign the elusive Nomo in 1995. For Murakami, Nomo's U.S. debut brought back many fond memories. But there are some memories he would like to forget.

"I remember flying into California on the DC-8 plane for the first time and how very beautiful it was," said Murakami, recalling his first trip to the Bay Area. I didn't know much about America at the time. I saw San Francisco. I saw Disneyland. My eyes were open big."

For Murakami there were no shoe contracts or ESPN highlights, as there would be for Nomo. Like Nomo, however, there was a language barrier he had to endure. "I did not speak much English, so I couldn't understand what anyone in the crowd was saying. I just tried to get batters out," says Murakami, who has been a Japanese television commentator for each of Nomo's starts. On August 5, 1995, the same day Nomo threw a one-hitter against the Giants, Murakami was honored at home plate in Candlestick Park to commemorate the thirtieth anniversary of his final year with the San Francisco Giants.

Nomo's success has generated a new interest in Murakami's brief career. At age 51 he is a broad-shouldered and handsome man who managed to toss some big league batting practice for the Giants while visiting here. "It all went by so fast," he says. Sadly, the Murakami experiment caused a veritable international incident that might have ruined a brilliant career. And this factor, more than anything else, best explains the three-decade hiatus between Murakami and Nomo to the big league scene.

Murakami, who was born in 1944, was of a different era indeed. Nineteen-sixty-four was less than 20 years after V-J Day. What this meant was an occasional ballpark drunk would taunt Murakami with racial slurs and reminders of who had won the war. But this was very much the exception rather than the rule, he insists. "It happened a couple of times," Murakami recalls. "I just listened and ignored them. If I said something, maybe people would get mad."

He grew up in the small town of Otsuki, and

learned to play baseball in the rice paddies with a tennis ball and a bamboo stick. Murakami had been pitching for the Nankai Hawks in Japan when the Giants discovered that his baffling curve ball could be beneficial to a team that was still a relatively newcomer to the Bay Area, a region with a heavy Asian-American population.

A Giant scout in Tokyo convinced Murakami's team in Nankai that it should send him and two teammates to the Giants for spring training, "to learn baseball the American way." The other players did not pan out, but the Giants were impressed enough by Murakami's work to keep him with the big club. The Giants said they would pay the Nankai team $10,000 if Murakami made the team.

The Giants sent him to Fresno for minor league seasoning, where he immediately experienced an inevitable clash of cultures. He was just 19 years old when he first rode the buses to California League cities with the Fresno club. He recalls being nervous about ordering a "chicken basket" because it might consist of cooked wicker—an actual basket—and he might have to eat it. Another time in Fresno, he once saluted a third baseman who made a good play behind him by running over and bowing to the infielder, cap doffed. It was at

51

Fresno that he picked up the nickname "Mashy" because his teammates had trouble pronouncing Masanori.

He was also a sensation at Fresno. "He was too good for the league," his Fresno manager, Bill Werle, said. He had an 11–7 record, a 1.78 ERA, and was named rookie of the year. When the Giants called him up in August 1964, he made his major league debut against the New York Mets at Shea Stadium. Murakami pitched 11 scoreless innings before any big league team got a run off him. He struck out four batters for every one he walked. He struck out Hank Aaron, and the Japanese-American community of the Bay Area embraced him.

After the season the Nankai team cried foul. They announced they were recalling him to Japan for the 1965 season, contending that the Pacific League only agreed to release him for a year. After threatened suits and counter suits, in April 1965 Japanese Commissioner Yushi Uchimura sent a lengthy letter to Commissioner Ford Frick announcing that Nankai had made a "grave mistake" and had not fully understood the terms of the original agreement. The Nankai club would allow Murakami to pitch for the Giants in 1965 and then be free to pitch wherever he wanted the next year.

Murakami made 45 appearances for the Giants in 1965, saving games for the likes of Juan Marichal and Gaylord Perry. He put together a 4–1 record, a 3.75 ERA, with 88 strikeouts and 22 walks. Pressured by his parents and the Hawks, he returned to Japan for 1966.

After his return he pitched 17 more seasons, accumulating 103 wins and 30 saves. But even today there are some who have not forgotten. On a recent visit to a senior citizens' center in San Francisco's Japantown, a 77-year-old woman was waiting. She showed Murakami a handkerchief that he had autographed for her in 1965 at a nearby restaurant where she'd been a waitress.

Masanori Murakami's two-year stint was over three years before Hideo Nomo was born. By the time Nomo played on the Japanese Olympic baseball team, which won the silver medal at Seoul, Korea, in 1988, Japanese baseball had assumed a larger interest in the United States. And while American kids were cheering the likes of Hank Aaron and Brooks Robinson, Hideo Nomo and his friends were cheering the exploits of the legendary Sadaharu Oh, Japan's answer to Babe Ruth.

On June 1, 1974, the *New York Times* introduced Sadaharu Oh to the American baseball public by reporting his 600th career home run. Oh became the subject of a great deal of American press and was consequently perceived by American fans almost exclusively as a home run hitter. Over his professional career with the Yomiuri Giants of Tokyo (1959–1980), Sadaharu Oh hit 868 career home runs. Yet he was far from a one-dimensional hitter. He did win fifteen Central League home run championships (including thirteen in a row), but he also led the league in batting five times, in RBIs thirteen times, and in runs scored fifteen times. In 1973 and 1974 young Hideo Nomo had lots to cheer about as Sadaharu Oh won back-to-back triple crowns.

But Oh's impact on the young Nomo was more than just extraordinary numbers, and a slew of unbreakable records. It was Oh's sense of professionalism, a code of discipline and spirituality about Sadaharu Oh that dignified both the man and the ballplayer.

Sadaharu Oh discussed his philosophy and thoughts with writer David Falkner in his 1985 autobiography. He is not Babe Ruth or Hank Aaron, he insists. "I can not compare myself to them any more than they have compared themselves with me. I am the Japanese Oh Sadaharu." The two figures who were his inspirations throughout his career were Lou Gehrig and the legendary Japanese samurai Miyamoto Musashi. Of Lou Gehrig, Oh says, "His physical body betrayed him. His spirit never did."

For Sadaharu Oh, baseball was more than a sport or a way to earn a living. "Baseball was for me, too, a form of spirit discipline, a way to make myself a better person—although I surely never sought discipline for such a reason. It became my Way, as the tea ceremony or flower arranging or making of poems were the Ways of others."

Professionalism was the one quality that was Sadaharu Oh's guiding star, and it has not been lost to Nomo. "I am a professional ballplayer," Oh told himself before playing the final game of his 22-year career in 1980. "A professional. The word has meaning for me as few others in my vocabulary do. There is a standard of performance you must maintain. It is best that you are able to give and then more—and to maintain that at a level of consistency. No excuses for the demands of your ego or the extremes of your emotions. It is an inner thing. I held myself to that standard for twenty-two years. It is my proudest achievement."

In 1989, nine years after Sadaharu Oh retired from Japanese baseball, nineteen-year-old Hideo Nomo became the first draft choice of the Kintetsu Buffaloes. According to public statements, the thought of one day playing baseball in the United States did not enter Nomo's mind until 1992, when he pitched against an All-Star team that was visiting Japan. "When I saw Roger Clemens pitching, he became my hero. But I gave no thought of pitching in America when I was growing up." However, some writers close to him say that from his early boyhood days, Nomo had dreams of one day playing baseball in the big leagues.

Either way, imagine the thrill when Nomo pitched for the Japanese All-Stars in 1992, and worked against his idol Roger Clemens. There's a tinge of irony as well. Three years later, when Hideo Nomo was making his historic All-Star Game start for the National League, it was Roger Clemens who was sitting at home admiring Nomo.

In Japan, Nomo's exploits were startling. In 1990, his rookie year with the Buffaloes, he set the Pacific League on fire. Appearing in 29 games, he led the league in wins (18), in earned run average (2.91), and strikeouts (287). He became an immediate all-star, and was the starting pitcher for the Japanese All-Stars against a touring group of American stars. He gave up one run in three innings, as his squad defeated the American team and Red Sox pitcher Dennis "Oil Can" Boyd by a score of 4–1. Pitching for the American team that day as well was Randy Johnson, Nomo's 1995 All-Star Game opponent. When reminded of this earlier encounter, Johnson admits that his thoughts are a bit vague. "That was five years ago, and I don't remember much except his delivery. But just the appearance of Nomo should bring some excitement to the game."

Nomo was chosen the 1990 Rookie of the Year in Japan and was awarded the coveted Saramura Prize, the Japanese equivalent of the Cy Young Award. And he kept right on rolling. For three more years he led the Pacific League in both wins and in strikeouts: 17–11, 287 K's (1991); 18–8, 228 K's (1992); and 17–12, 275 K's (1993). He reached the 1,000 strikeout mark faster than anyone in Japanese baseball history. Five times he made the Pacific League All-Star team. In Japan they called him "Dr. K" as Dwight Gooden was called here in the United States.

Yet Nomo's hope of testing himself in the major leagues hit a snag in 1994. A shoulder problem limited him to just 17 games and a subpar record of 8–7. But there was still no denying his staggering numbers the past five years with the Buffaloes. In that five-year span he had won 78 games and lost 46. Four times he had led the league in wins and strikeouts. His earned run average was a very respectable 3.15. Not counting his injury-ridden 1994, he averaged 270 strikeouts in 234 innings. Translated to the extreme, this comes to 1.16 strike-outs an inning and 8.9 strikeouts per game during his four injury-free years.

His dreams of big league baseball aside, what finally lured Hideo Nomo to America is a story in itself. Worried that he was being overused by the Buffaloes, he hired a personal trainer and resisted his manager's traditional Japanese thinking about pitching through pain. Those close to Japanese baseball agree—and statistics bear this out—that Nomo was worried that he would burn his arm out quickly in Japan, where starting pitchers are often allowed to throw 190 pitches a game, nearly twice the standard in the United States.

There was another pressing factor. He was tired of playing for a non-winner and requested that the Buffaloes trade him after the season. When they refused, he hired Don Nomura, an agent with close ties to the major leagues. Nomura's stepfather, Katsuga, was the manager of the Yakurito Swallows in Japan. Nomo then proceeded to retire from Japanese baseball. This allowed him to escape Japan's ten-year service minimum for free agency, thus permitting him to negotiate with U.S. teams. Japanese contracts restrict a retiring player from playing for other Japanese clubs only, a loophole Nomo fully used to his advantage.

On January 9, 1995, Hideo Nomo announced his retirement. On January 30, he and his agent left for the United States with the purpose of negotiating a major league contract. The Seattle Mariners became the first club to announce that they were planning to give Nomo a physical checkup. In early February *Sports Illustrated* reported that Nomo had said he would negotiate with seven clubs, including the Mariners. The other clubs included the Giants, Dodgers, Yankees, Braves and Marlins.

The Giants were particularly interested. So eager, in fact, that they did all they could to lure Nomo to the City by the Bay. Representatives from the Giants, including manager Dusty Baker, courted Nomo with a dinner in San Francisco early in the month. According to Baker, "Don Nomura did most of the talking, Nomo did most of the eating." San Francisco Giant owner Peter Magowan even enlisted the help of the Japanese consulate, and former Japanese star Masanori Murakami was also called upon to help lure Nomo into the Giants' fold. It was to no avail. In pure dollars and cents, the Giants refused to come up with the kind of cash offered by the Los Angeles Dodgers. "How do you make an evaluation on somebody you haven't seen pitch?" a frustrated Dusty Baker said. "It shows that [the Dodgers] have more money than us. They can take a chance. This is probably what you call a speculative investment. 'Wildcatting,' " he called it.

On February 13, 1995, Nomo signed a contract with the Los Angeles Dodgers. All future stops were canceled, including one in Atlanta. According to Dodger manager Tommy Lasorda, Nomo had always wanted to pitch for the Dodgers. But there has been some contention otherwise. The Braves wanted him, according to general manager John Scheurholz, who claimed that if the Dodger offer had come up short, Nomo would have been on his way to Atlanta. Nomo himself says that the Braves lost interest in him and simply didn't project him as a starting pitcher.

"Absurd," countered Scheurholz. Atlanta wanted Nomo all along, but the Dodgers "never gave them a chance." Perhaps the real answer rests somewhere in between. But if there is any truth to the Atlanta contention, imagine for a moment a starting rotation with Greg Maddux, Tom Glavine, John Smoltz, and Hideo Nomo.

Speculation and second-guessing aside, the truth is that Nomo was a natural for the Los Angeles Dodgers in more ways than one. Texas

Ranger general manager Doug Melvin recognized this early on. "If Nomo signs with a team on the West Coast, where there is a huge Asian population," Melvin commented, "we could see the Nipponese Valenzuela soon after the strike gets settled. He's got a great forkball, and he's still young. No matter where he signs, we're sure to see a new standard Japanese player contract."

But just how high that standard would be set had yet to be established. Hideo Nomo was going to play major league baseball in the United States. How well he would succeed was still an unanswered question.

# 4

# Welcome Aboard, Mr. Nomo

"**N**ewest Dodger" was the title of a *Los Angeles Times* editorial on February 16, 1995.

The editorial went on to say, "Japanese fans are likely to become Dodger fans as they track star pitcher Hideo Nomo, who is leaving Osaka for the Los Angeles team. . . . The 6 foot 2, 210 pound pitcher is nicknamed "The Tornado" in Japan because of his zany corkscrew windup. . . . Nomo's acculturation to baseball American style will be interesting to observe. American and Japanese play by almost the same rules, but with very different philosophies."

The news conference the Dodgers called to announce the signing of Hideo Nomo was far from typical. But few would argue that the Dodgers have ever been a typical baseball organization. To the contrary, they usually pride themselves on being baseball pioneers.

It was the Dodgers who hired the major leagues' first black player, Jackie Robinson, and later the first black pitcher, Dan Bankhead, in 1947. Then it was the great Don Newcombe, who anchored the Dodger staff in the early and mid 1950s. The Dodgers had a great Jewish pitcher in Sandy Koufax during the 1960s, and a great Mexican pitcher by the name of Fernando Valenzuela in the 1980s. So what could be more fitting than the possibility of a great Japanese pitcher in the 1990s? Moreover, by signing Nomo to a Dodger contract, owner Peter O'Malley realized the fruition of a dream he had harbored since he had accompanied his father, Walter, and the Brooklyn Dodgers on a goodwill tour of Japan in 1956.

The Nomo news conference more resembled a Hollywood premier than a baseball gathering. The aroma was that of sushi and teriyaki chicken, not the scent of hot dogs and peanuts. Men wore Bally shoes and European suits, not jeans and sneakers. Fifteen camera crews were at the back of the ballroom, while two dozen photographers jostled for position in front. About 200 people sat at tables adorned with miniature Japanese and American flags. Even with a strike in progress, a canceled World Series, and the uncertainty of a 1995 season opener, the signing of Hideo Nomo was a media delight, a resplendent affair worthy of Hollywood glitz and glamour. It transcended the baseball diamond in the United States and was major headline news in Japan.

"This is very big news in our country," said Hiroto Shiba, a reporter for the Nikkon Sports News. "I know it's not a big story in the United States, maybe because they don't know him, but he's a big star in Japan." With every compliment uttered by Dodger owner Peter O'Malley, and with every word uttered by Nomo, Japanese reporters and dignitaries responded with a salvo of applause. Nomo added to the allure of the moment by autographing Dodger paraphernalia for his many well-wishers.

Intriguingly, O'Malley offered Nomo a $2 million signing bonus to go along with his $109,000 minimum salary, even though no one in the Dodger organization had seen Nomo pitch except in a two-minute video. In fact, Nomo's only workout with the Dodgers to date had consisted of playing catch for seven minutes with pitching coach Dave Wallace.

Only after they signed Nomo did the Dodgers

acquire his complete pitching records from Japan. What they saw stunned them. The records showed that Nomo had thrown more than 140 pitches in a game 61 times. In one game he walked 16 batters and threw 198 pitches. In another game he threw 191 pitches. Some people in the Dodger camp were deeply concerned. "It's crazy," one organization person was heard to mutter. "I've never heard of such pitch counts. It makes you worry. You wonder how much he has left."

Yes, there were doubters. The bad shoulder and Nomo's control problems were well known. His success came as a pleasant surprise. "Frankly speaking, no one imagined such a great achievement," said Masaru Ikei, a professor of political science at Keio University, who described himself as "a crazy baseball fan." One Japanese manager predicted that Nomo would fail because he threw too many *foa boru*, a Japanese term for walks. Even the sagely Murakami sold Nomo a bit short, saying at the start of the season that even if Nomo worked his way into the Dodger starting rotation, he wouldn't be able to win more than ten games.

However, one thing was very clear. By signing Nomo to a Dodger contract, O'Malley helped to foster the internationalization of baseball. This had always been dear to his heart. It had been nearly fifty years since Branch Rickey and the Brooklyn Dodgers broke baseball's longstanding color line by signing Jackie Robinson. Soon the Latin connection was firmly established when Minnie Minoso, Roberto Clemente, Luis Aparicio, and Orlando Cepeda became the early pioneers for future Latin players.

Now there was Hideo Nomo. It didn't matter much that baseball was still on strike, or that disgust with the game was at an all-time high. It didn't seem to matter much either that Nomo had had a sore arm the previous year when tendinitis in his right shoulder limited him to just 114 innings, or that several other teams had backed away from him, contending that his shoulder was still sore. What did matter was that for twenty-six-year-old Hideo Nomo from Osaka, Japan, the first part of a dream had come true. The eyes, ears, and cameras of two nations were on him in full focus. The hard work was about to begin.

Nomo wasn't even eligible for a place on the Dodger roster at first. Because of the baseball strike, the Department of Labor would not permit any foreigners to serve as replacement players. The best he could do was to go to Triple A and return to the majors when the strike was settled. There was much at stake, and Nomo knew it.

"Even if [the strike] ends, I have no guarantee of playing in the major leagues. So it's vital for me to do well in camp," he said through his interpreter. And there was some validity to his concern. Yukata Enatsu—one of Japan's greatest pitchers ever—tried unsuccessfully to make the Milwaukee Brewers in 1985 at age 37. Enatsu, who holds the Japanese record with 401 strikeouts in a season and won 25 games in 1968, made it to the final cut but decided to quit rather than play in the minors.

From the start, Nomo fully realized how large the stakes were. "Japanese players can't come to the United States and play in the majors," Nomo said through his interpreter. "I'm the only one who has broken through the rules. I have to do my best and pitch well in the major leagues. If the result is good, young Japanese players will follow me."

Now a full-fledged member of the Dodger organization, Nomo headed home to Japan to get his working visa. When he left Japan to join the Dodgers on the last day of February, it was not without great trepidation. As he tried to fall asleep at his Osaka home, his mind churned through the night. He tried lying on his left side, then his right, his back and then his stomach. It was an ordeal. His eyes constantly darted to the clock. Just before dawn he sat up and chills ran through his body. In a few hours he would be leaving on a plane for another continent, and to a strange country where he had no family or friends.

He looked back at the many conversations he had over the past few months, the consternation of friends when he told them of his plans. He was told by many with whom he was closest, that he was stupid. His parents were disconcerted. They responded as if he had joined a religious cult. Even his wife, Kikuko, the only person in whom he could confide his dreams, had difficulty accepting his decision. He was a baseball star in Japan with plenty of money, a fancy house, and luxury cars. He was one of the most famous athletes in the country. He was courting the possibility of failure, and personally setting back the cause of Japanese baseball.

He knew his family life had been permanently altered. For the past month his picture had been on the front page of every Japanese sports publication. His wife and his three-year-old son, Takahiro, had lost their privacy. He was going to a foreign country without knowing the language. He would miss his family dearly, and there would be many days of loneliness. He also took a sizable pay cut from his $2 million salary in Japan to sign for the major league minimum. He was following a dream, but he faced the risk of sacrificing everything: money, family, and even his career should he fail.

Moreover, his departure from Japan was not without controversy. Although most people wished him success, some felt that he had betrayed Japanese baseball by taking advantage of a loophole in the rules. But such feelings were shortlived. By leaving Japan and showing that a Japanese player could succeed in America, Nomo has given a bigger boost to Japanese baseball than he ever could have done by staying.

"It's my life, and that's the only way I can look at it," he recalled saying. "I knew what the risks were. I knew everybody was watching me. But I also knew that if I didn't do this, I would spend the rest of my life regretting it."

He knew the score when he joined the Dodgers in Vero Beach, Florida. "The American interest in me is because I am from Japan. Now I'd like to let them know that I can compete on this level as myself, as Hideo Nomo."

Hoffman Stadium in Vero Beach, Florida, is the spring training home of the Los Angeles Dodgers. It is part of a 450-acre complex known since 1965 as Dodgertown. Surrounding Hoffman Stadium are two and a half practice fields, a long row of batting cages with pitching machines, two golf courses, a clubhouse, a restaurant, a lounge open to the public, a pro shop, swimming pools, tennis courts, a recreation room, and a movie theater for Dodger personnel. There is also a 70-acre citrus grove. The half field is for infield practice, bunting practice, etc.

When Nomo joined the club in Vero Beach, the Los Angeles Dodgers had 103 foreign players in their system, 19 of whom were on their 40-man roster. In fact, the pitching staff had a United Nations stamp of sorts: Ramon Martinez and Pedro Astacio from the Dominican Republic, Ismael Valdes from Mexico, and Chan Ho Park from Korea. Of the potential starters, Tom Candiotti was one of the few Americans. Because of the team's diversity, Nomo felt a bit more comfortable than he might have otherwise.

"When I came to Florida, I was a little nervous," Nomo was quoted as saying. "But my teammates treat me very well. And the good thing about the Dodgers is that they don't have just American-born players. They have players from all over the world. That's one of the reasons why I am comfortable. But I know it has become difficult for my family. It is very difficult to get about these days."

At first he felt isolated in the clubhouse. Despite the robust clubhouse clamor, he sat conspicuously alone as his teammates amused themselves with such familiar bits of Americana as CD players and heavy metal music, NBA games on TV, and box scores in the Sunday edition. Nomo's favorite pop artist is Motoharu Sano, a famous rock musician in Japan. To help him relax he had brought some tapes of Sano with him.

Initially, though, his biggest problem was not the clash of cultures, or the language handicap (the first American expression he learned from his teammates was "Hey, dude"). What bothered him most was the assault on his privacy. According to Michael Okurmura, his interpreter and baseball's first full-time translator, it started instantly in spring training.

As soon as he arrived, 30 Japanese reporters were waiting in the wings. Within days he accused the Japanese media of writing misleading stories, particularly about his arm. Nomo insisted he had recovered completely from the injuries that had plagued him in 1994.

Like his American counterparts, Nomo wanted the press to restrict its reporting to his performance on the field. "They write too many private things," he told the *Los Angeles Times*. "They're like the paper I see at the checkout counter. You know, the one they call the *National Enquirer*. So I'm checking on what those guys are writing about me. If that happens again, I don't ever want them to write about me." Soon he limited his interviews to one every four days.

Nomo's problems with the Japanese media far predated his arrival at Vero Beach. At first the Dodgers were a little alarmed at the apparent hostilities. Most Japanese media people considered him to be a rude boor. It was not exactly what the Dodger public relations people had anticipated. Sure, he was a star in Japan, but he had been a media recluse.

Much of this stemmed from winning Rookie of the Year in 1990. After that season he became engaged to his wife, Kikuko. Then unpleasant instances started. Wherever they went, photographers were waiting. It angered him greatly when he saw their pictures in every tabloid and magazine on the checkout counter. Editors were craving stories, and Nomo was big-time news. They couldn't write much about a man who wasn't talking. It took months for reporters even to find out what his father did in Osaka. (He is a postman.) Relations became so strained with the Japanese press that during the early spring, after the strike had ended and South Korean pitcher Chan Ho Park came to camp at Vero Beach, Japanese reporters were openly rooting for Park.

By becoming a Dodger, Nomo became a part of the National League's most successful franchise, on both the East and West coast, and whose roots were planted way in the nineteenth century.

The borough of Brooklyn was represented by many teams in baseball's early days, including the Eckfords, Excelsiors, Atlantics, Bridegrooms, Superbas, Trolley Dodgers, Robins (after their manager, Wilbert Robinson), and finally the Dodgers.

In 1912, Dodger owner Charles Ebbets was convinced that his team's fortunes would improve if it had a new park. The site he picked was a garbage dump called Pigtown in Flatbush, one of the poorest sections of the borough. He built his park, complete with a marble rotunda and chandeliers, for $750,000, a sum so large that he had to sell half his interest in the team to pay his debts.

Ebbets Field officially opened to the public on April 13, 1913, with an exhibition game against the New York Highlanders, who officially changed their name to the Yankees that spring. Brooklyn won 3 to 2, thanks to an inside-the-park home run by a young outfielder and former dental student from Kansas City named Charles Dillon Stengel, whom his teammates would soon start calling by the more familiar name of Casey.

The Brooklyn Dodgers won their first National League flag in 1916 and their second four years later in 1920. Both times they were beaten in the World Series, first by the Boston Red Sox and then by the Cleveland Indians.

Between 1921 and 1939 the Brooklyn Dodgers were among the National League's perennial doormats, enjoying only six winning seasons and four first-division finishes in those years. But with the onset of World War II, as defense production was stimulated and the Depression began to wane, their fortunes changed. In the late thirties, the Dodgers went from perennial sixth-placers to perennial pennant contenders.

In 1941 the Dodgers won 100 games and their third National League pennant, losing the World Series in five games to the hated Yankees. In 1942 they won a team record 104 games (broken in 1953) yet finished second, two games behind the world champion St. Louis Cardinals. Brooklyn sure loved their "Bums," and at the end of World War II the Dodgers put together one of the most exciting arrays of baseball talent ever assembled on any diamond.

From 1947 through 1956 they won six National League pennants, with such names as Robinson, Reese, Snider, Hodges, Campanella, and Furillo, becoming forever enshrined in baseball lore. They came preciously close again in 1950, when they were beaten by the "Whiz Kids" from Philadelphia on the last day of the season. And of course in 1951 Leo Durocher's New York Giants and Bobby Thomson's "shot heard around the world" snatched still another NL title from their grasp. But every year except 1955, they were beaten in the World Series by the crosstown New York Yankees, managed by a fellow named Casey Stengel, who once upon a time had played right field for them.

In 1958 the name O'Malley instantly became synonymous with high treason in Flatbush as Walter O'Malley left Brooklyn and headed westward to Los Angeles with his Dodgers. A new era in baseball was on the horizon. The same year Horace Stoneham moved the New York Giants from its ancient home in the Polo Grounds to San Francisco.

Since moving to Los Angeles, the Dodgers have captured nine National League titles and five world championships. Moreover, in a sport where managers crumble as quickly as yesterday's cake, the Dodgers have had only two managers in the past

41 years. Walter Alston became Dodger skipper in 1954 in Brooklyn, headed west with the team in 1958, and stayed at the helm until 1976. One of baseball's most successful managers, Alston put together a record of 2,040 wins and 1,613 losses. Tommy Lasorda was named manager in 1976 and reigns today as baseball's most enduring skipper.

When Hideo Nomo signed with the Dodgers, it is questionable whether he knew how well rookies had fared in the organization. Since 1947, when Jackie Robinson captured the first Rookie of the Year Award, Dodger rookies won 14 Rookie of the Year awards. Among them were Nomo's would-be teammates Eric Karros, Mike Piazza, and Raul Mondesi, who won the award in 1992, 1993, and 1994 respectively. If Nomo could win it in 1995, it would be four in a row for the Los Angeles Dodgers.

But such thoughts were a long way off. The job at hand now for Nomo was to make the team, then prove to the Dodgers that he could win, and win big as a major league pitcher.

# 5

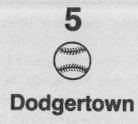

# Dodgertown

In early 1995 there was an air of excitement in the Miyako Hotel in San Francisco's Japantown. A whole generation of younger Japanese Americans were talking Nomo. These are the Sanseis, the third generation of Japanese Americans whose grandparents immigrated to the United States. "We were all very excited when we heard the Giants were trying to sign him," says Karen Kinoshita, director of catering at the Miyako. "In this community you didn't have to follow the papers, because there was always someone that did. The excitement was incredible. You could see it building."

Similar feelings were expressed by Michael Kuo, a technical coordinator for Pacific Leisure Management in San Francisco. "I have Japanese friends who are students here. Since Nomo first signed with the Dodgers, they have been following his every move."

But when the Dodgers signed him, few could have imagined that he would be the National League's All-Star Game starting pitcher. Or that he would be leading the senior circuit in strikeouts, would be second to Greg Maddux in earned run average, and would limit opposing hitters to a major league low .165 batting average.

In addition to his enormous pitching skills, Nomo was fortunate. Critics might have been dubious about the soundness of his right arm. They may have been dubious about his straight fastball, his control, and his ability to adopt to a different culture. Some thought he might crumble under the pressure of having to pitch for an entire season, and being followed every day by a huge pack of journalists.

One National League star who grew to respect Nomo greatly was Tony Gwynn. Gwynn especially appreciated Nomo's ability to deal with the vast barrage of media hype. "The thing which impresses me the most [about Nomo] is with all that hoopla and all these people following him, he has remained level-headed and kept his composure,"

Gwynn says. "To me, from a pitcher's standpoint, that is important. Because when you are a guy out on the hill, surrounded by people, surrounded by hype, and can keep your composure like that, you have a sense of what kind of competitor he is."

From the start Nomo received great support from Dodger manager Tommy Lasorda and from owner Peter O'Malley. "When he came to Vero Beach, I told our coaches that I didn't want nobody trying to change him," Lasorda said. "His windup didn't bother me. Luis Tiant got hitters out with that windup." Not since Tiant, in fact, had baseball seen such an unorthodox delivery. However, the Dodgers were concerned enough about Nomo's herky-jerky pitching motion that they brought in Ed Vargo, the National League's umpire-in-chief, to take a look. "It's no big deal, just needs some fine tuning," Vargo said after watching Nomo work out.

His form was exciting. Nomo would throw his arms straight up while thrusting his chest forward. After holding the pose for a second, he'd turn sharply toward second base, with his back to the batter. Then he whirled forward to deliver his pitch—a splendid assortment of curveballs, fork-balls, and a fastball clocked at 92 mph. The Dodgers did make one adjustment to his high-kick, corkscrew delivery. At first he would start and stop similar to Luis Tiant. The Dodgers eliminated the double stopping, which would lead him to balk, but the windup remained the same. It was his own style. It was the way he was most effective. And it worked.

Peter O'Malley's concern for Nomo was especially rewarding. He kept a close watch every time Nomo took to the mound during the spring, either in a game or in batting practice. "He's trying to do something never done—it's an extraordinary challenge. I'm spending a lot of time with him, as though he's my own son. He's here from another continent. The food, the setting, they're all totally different. I'm trying to make him feel as much at home as possible. . . . I'm a believer in trends, and his trend is definitely positive."

From the start one of Nomo's biggest boosters was Fred Claire, the Dodgers' executive vice president. He was certain that Nomo was a major league pitcher. It was more than the potential strikeouts and shutouts. What impressed Claire most was Nomo's pioneering spirit and his great courage, particularly during the hectic contract negotiations.

"Here you are, one of the most successful pitchers in Japan, one of the most famous and making

more money and having the opportunity to con-
tinue to make more money over there. You're way
up here. You've already done that. You have all
that, and you're literally willing to put it on the
table and risk it."

What bothered Nomo most was being viewed as
a curiosity. Persistent Japanese journalists made
him so press-weary during spring training, according to *Sports Illustrated*'s Tom Verducci, that Nomo
agreed to field questions from *Sports Illustrated* only
after receiving the promise "not to sell your story
to the Japanese media." The problem became so
acute that in late August, after Nomo dropped
three of four starts, Lasorda made it clear that the
band of 50 or so journalists who traveled with the
Dodgers might well be taking too much of a toll on
his rookie pitcher.

With the 1995 season on the horizon, many
Japanese papers were reporting that Nomo had
made the Dodger roster. On April 9, the *Los
Angeles Times* noted that Nomo might well have
won a job in the starting rotation. "Nomo, who
was unable to pitch off a mound until three weeks
ago, dazzled everyone in the first intrasquad game,
pitching two perfect innings. He struck out two
and allowed only one ball to be hit to the outfield."

"I'd like to be the fourth or fifth starter, but

I'm just one of many who want the chance. I'm confident." These were Nomo's words after his first springtime exhibition appearance against the Florida Marlins on April 13. His first spring training encounter was promising but rather unremarkable.

When he entered the game with one out in the fifth inning, he promptly walked three straight Marlins. He got himself out of the jam, first with a strikeout, then a line drive to left to retire the side. The next inning he was far more composed. He struck out two of the three batters he faced. In his two innings of work, he faced nine batters without allowing a hit. He threw 42 pitches, walking three and striking out three.

"Nervous? Of course he was nervous, and you're the guys who make him nervous with all those cameras," Tommy Lasorda said to the large group of Japanese media hovering close to Nomo. "This was a big day. He was very impressive, especially the way he got out of the jam."

Nomo would make two more spring training appearances: on April 17 against the New York Yankees, and on April 22 against the Marlins. His main problem was control. Against the Yankees he went four innings. He faced 16 batters, allowed just one hit, walked three, and struck out one.

Against the Marlins, he gave up four hits in five innings, walking three and striking out five. His native country of Japan was taking notice, prompting Tommy Lasorda to say in Japanese, *"Nomo wa ii-mono ne!"* (Nomo is good, isn't he?)

The year 1995 was not a good one for Japan. In some ways it paralleled 1968 in the United States. Only instead of raucous anti-war protests, massive social unrest, and errant political conventions, Japan was beset with such problems as the Kobe earthquake, terrorists unleashing nerve gas in the Tokyo subway, and a hijacker holding a crowded jumbo jet hostage for fifteen hours. Worse still, beyond the terrorism and the destruction and loss of life caused by the January earthquake, the economy had reentered a recession, and there was growing concern about unemployment.

While Japan was experiencing its share of natural and human disaster, baseball in the United States seemed to be self-destructing on its own. An eight-month strike and the cancellation of the World Series—the first time since 1904 that the October classic had been put on hold—stupefied and angered the American baseball public. Baseball needed a shot in the arm. The Orioles' Cal Ripken, Jr., would supply some of the serum by surpassing Lou Gehrig's "Iron Man" record. Yet baseball needed something new and different. Waiting in the wings to fill this void was Hideo Nomo.

In 1994, baseball had been realigned for the first time since 1969. Much to the chagrin of traditionalists, the expanding markets necessitated three divisions for both the National and American leagues. For the first time ever in the big-league history, a second-place or "wildcard" team could possibly win everything. This factor in itself promised to benefit the Dodgers in the strike-shortened season of 1995.

The Dodgers were already the preseason favorites to take the four-team N.L. West, a division including the San Francisco Giants, San Diego Padres, and upstart Colorado Rockies. The Dodgers had been leading the West in 1994 when the strike cut the season short.

With catcher Mike Piazza and outfielder Raul Mondesi, the Dodgers had two of the game's great young players. Piazza, who put together a .318 average, 35 homers, and 112 RBIs in his rookie season of 1993, followed it up in 1994 with another great year (.319, 24 HR, and 92 RBI). Mondesi was the unanimous choice as National League Rookie of the Year in 1994, hitting .306 with 16 homers and 56 RBIs. Many old-timers were saying that Mondesi could well be the most complete player to come into the game in many years, with a right-field throwing arm comparable to such greats as Carl Furillo and Roberto Clemente.

Moreover, in first baseman Eric Karros the Dodgers had the 1992 National League Rookie of the Year. Karros had more than 20 home runs and 80 runs batted in 1992 and 1993, but slipped to .266, 14 HR, and 46 RBI in 1994. (In 1995 Karros would have a banner year, belting 32 homers and leading the club with 105 RBIs.) Third baseman Tim Wallach, an outstanding player with the Montreal Expos for many years, had been the National League's Comeback Player of the Year with the Dodgers in 1994. Second baseman Delino De-Shields, whom the Dodgers obtained late in 1993, was a proven base stealer who had blossomed into one of the game's better players.

Traditionally the Dodgers have had quality pitching. Often when their bats failed, their pitching kept them afloat. Since Don Newcombe first won the Cy Young Award in 1956, the Dodgers have had seven Cy Young winners, the last being Orel Hershhheiser in 1988. It was a worthy legacy that included Sandy Koufax, Don Drysdale, and Fernando Valenzuela.

There was another factor working in their favor. Since their last-place finish in 1992, the Dodgers had been in a process of rebuilding. That year they lost 99 games to become cellar dwellers for the first time since 1905. Only knuckleball pitcher Tom Candiotti and former 20-game winner Ramon Martinez were proven starters. Ismael Valdes was 3–1 in 1994. A 21-year-old right-hander from the Dominican Republic, Valdes became Nomo's best friend during the spring. "I got to know him in spring training," Valdes said. "He's law-abiding. He doesn't get into trouble. He's quiet. I like that kind of person."

On April 28, Nomo made his U.S. debut by pitching for Bakersfield (CA) at Rancho Cucamonga. He allowed six hits in 5⅓ innings, walking one and striking out six. He got a standing ovation as he left the field. By starting the last week of the season in the minors, however, Nomo was deprived of becoming the nineteenth player that year to make his professional debut in the major leagues.

During the abbreviated spring training, Nomo was 2–0, allowing five hits and two runs, one earned, in 11 innings of work. He walked nine and struck out nine. The Dodgers had seen enough to put him in the starting rotation. On May 2, 26-year-old Hideo Nomo would get his first big-league start in against the San Francisco Giants at Candlestick Park.

# 6

# The No-Decision Man

"**T**he Start of Something Big? We proudly hail the Hideo Nomo diamond dynasty. So mark down this date in Dodger baseball history," wrote Mike Downey in the *Los Angeles Times*, the day after Nomo's historic debut.

It was high drama at Candlestick Park the night of May 2, 1995. Throngs of reporters and photographers packed the ballpark as Hideo Nomo took the mound. Although there were only 16,099 paying customers, scores of Far East journalists had thronged to Candlestick Park.

He arrived at the ball park in a white limousine with Tommy Lasorda and hitting coach Reggie Smith. When he reached the clubhouse he stayed by himself, listening to his portable cassette recorder. He had the hopes of an entire nation hanging on his right arm. In his native Japan he was in the media spotlight. His major league debut was telecast live at 4:30 A.M., and millions of Japanese were awake to watch it.

Ryozo Kato, the consul-general of Japan in San Francisco, was there. So were dozens of Japanese journalists, who were dispatched to the United States with the sole mandate to monitor Nomo's every move, every pitch. During his pregame exercises, more than 100 members of the Japanese news media gathered so close to Nomo that he needed San Francisco policemen to fend off their cameras. The mob continued into the clubhouse after the game.

"I've never seen so many Japanese press, so many Japanese cameras," said an astonished Tommy Lasorda. "Here we are in San Francisco, and they were filming him getting dressed. He has a whole following pulling for him closely, to see if they're good enough to play here. In this respect he's a trailblazer."

Cheers erupted the moment Nomo emerged from the Dodger dugout and walked to the mound. In Section 12 of Candlestick Park, well-wishers rose as one from their seats, unfurling the Japanese flag. The amount of press coverage to

Dodger games would become unprecedented, more so than in the early 1980s when Fernando Valenzuela held the spotlight. A new phenomena called "Nomo Mania" was in the making.

The *New York Times* captioned Nomo's debut: "Rookie in a League of His Own." For years the Japanese had watched American players cross the ocean to dominate their baseball. Usually they had been marginal players too old for the major leagues, or players not able to play regularly in the big show. Now Hideo Nomo had set out to prove to everyone that he could play baseball with the best in the world.

Roger Clemens may have been his model, but Nomo seemed more like a right-handed Randy Johnson in his debut against the Giants. Although he was bothered with control problems, when he got his pitches over the plate he was overpowering. In five scoreless innings he allowed one hit and struck out seven. With each new strikeout fans in right field held up signs with a big red K.

"I'm glad to see it," said Maki Sato, a Japanese native living in Menlo Park, California. "Baseball was taught by the American people, and finally we came back to say thank you."

Except for a nervous first inning, which caused Lasorda to pace and moan a bit, Nomo proved himself every bit a big league pitcher. But Lasorda's concern is easily understandable. It took Nomo 32 pitches and 20 minutes to get out of the first inning. After getting Darren Lewis on a called third strike and forcing Robbie Thompson to pop out to first, Nomo walked Barry Bonds, Matt Williams, and Glenallen Hill in succession. He then struck out Royce Clayton with an inside fastball. As Clayton fanned, a delighted fan behind first base could be seen waving a Japanese flag.

"I told him to relax and *hikuku*, keep the ball down, or at least that's what I think I said," commented pitching coach Dave Wallace, after making a trip to the mound helped to settle Nomo down. Nomo allowed the Giants only one hit, a third-inning double by Robbie Thompson off the left field wall. When he returned to the dugout after his final inning, his teammates bowed in unison.

"Nomo was absolutely brilliant in his major league debut," wrote Bob Nightengale in the *Los Angeles Times*. Of his 91 pitches, 52 were strikes. When he left the game after five innings, the score was tied 0–0. He would watch carefully for more than three hours before the Dodgers broke through with three runs in the top of the 15th. The Giants, though, rallied for four runs in the bottom of the 15th for a 4–3 Giant win.

Tommy Lasorda probably cursed his way when Matt Williams doubled home Barry Bonds with the winning run, but he liked what he saw when it came to Nomo. "What more can you say about what he did?" Lasorda said. "He pitched five innings and gave up one hit. I don't have to say how impressive it was."

The Giants' coach Wendell Kim was impressed with Nomo's assortment of pitches. "He's got a lot of pitches, people don't always realize this," Kim argues. "He's got a fastball that moves in and out. The split-finger forkball, or whatever you want to call it, it moves everywhere. He's got a slow curve which moves like a slider, and his change-up. So he's got four or five pitches."

San Francisco slugger Matt Williams recalled facing Nomo for the first time. "I remember he walked the bases loaded in the first inning. He walked Barry [Bonds], he walked me, and he walked Glenallen [Hill] with two outs, and then he ended up getting a strikeout to end the inning. With Nomo it's a question of hitting strikes against him. I'm not sure he's in his class, but he's almost a Greg Maddux because Maddux doesn't throw strikes, he gets you to swing at balls. The more patient you are, I think the better you handle a pitcher like that. The problem is that we're all taught to be aggressive. Often times your aggressiveness gets the best of you, especially with somebody like that."

Williams also says that Nomo's forkball is not the same as a split-finger. "Most guys use their split-finger mainly as an off-speed pitch, and it will dive because of lack of velocity. But a forkball is different in the sense that it will move. It doesn't only go down, but it will move, depending on how it is thrown like a knuckleball, because it has very little rotation."

Giant shortstop Royce Clayton would break up Nomo's no-hitter at Candlestick Park in August, but in early May he was mesmerized by Nomo. "I never saw anything like it," said Clayton, recalling his first at-bat. "It's something you never see in this league, and I never saw Luis Tiant. But it's not so much the motion, but what he has on the ball. He had great velocity. The guy throws a 92-94 mile fastball, and releases it from the exact location as he throws his split."

Former San Francisco fire chief Cal Hinton was one more person who was thrilled at the sight of Nomo. As a member of the Giants Senior program, the 68-year-old Hinton was working the series between the Giants and Dodgers when Nomo made his pitching debut.

"It was interesting," Cal Hinton recalls. "I've watched a lot of baseball, but I can't think of anyone who pitched that way. I remember when the other guy [Murakami] was here. It's been a long time, but I don't think his presentation was quite like this."

Someone on the other side of the ocean was even more delighted. Shizu Nomo told Japanese reporters at his home in Osaka that he was pleased with his son's debut. "I found out about his performance this morning. I was worried about how much my son could do, given everyone's expectations. But I'm relieved now to see that he could pitch his first game without much trouble."

Nomo was stoic throughout the game. Rarely did he show expression. Whatever his feelings, he camouflaged them well. But the next day he admitted to the *Los Angeles Times* that the game was the greatest thrill of his career. "I've been pitching since I was 16," he said. "But I never had a feeling like I did [Tuesday]. It was a very special feeling. It's one I will never forget. I've gone through a lot, but believe me, this was worth the wait."

Sportswriter Bob Nightengale noted in the *Los Angeles Times* that wherever you looked in Section 12 there were fans rooting for Nomo. One man wearing a Dodger cap was scheduled to return to Osaka from his Los Angeles business trip. Instead he rerouted his trip. His business at the Osaka Panasonic Plant could wait, he said. But Nomo couldn't! "I wanted to see this game very bad. This is a big day for all of us. I'm going to remember this day as long as I live. My ticket [stub], I'm going to take care of it very well."

Similarly, Katsuya Egawa and Souch Honda, both flight attendants stationed in the Napa Valley, California, told their bosses they couldn't possibly work that day. "You're kidding, there was no way we were going to miss this," Honda said. "This is something that one day we'll be able to tell our grandchildren about."

"This was a very, very big start," said Isao Shibata, former Japanese center fielder, who was at the game with a television crew. "How he performs shows how far Japanese baseball has come. By him being successful, it will open the door to Japanese people."

In Japan former San Francisco Giant Masanori Murakami was watching in the wee hours of the morning. A baseball commentator in his native country, Murakami watched Nomo's pitching debut with pride. "I'm very happy to see another Japanese after all these years. His performance brought back lots of fond memories for me. My heart was pumping for him."

San Francisco Giant owner Peter Magowan couldn't quite lure Nomo to the Giant camp a few months earlier. Now he was watching carefully. Was Magowan impressed? "Absolutely," he said. "I think he's going to be a draw. Maybe not the way Fernando [Valenzuela] was, but he's definitely going to be a draw. Not because he's Japanese, but because he's got such a unique and colorful way of pitching that is going to draw attention. People will see him on TV and will want to see him in person."

Giant manager Dusty Baker was equally impressed. "He's everything they built him up to be," said an admiring Baker. "He had the advantage of scouting reports on our hitters, but he's got good enough stuff to get people out the second or third time around."

On May 7 the glory that was Nomo's was put on momentary hold. The Colorado Rockies were only in the third year and already were becoming genuine contenders. They had a cast of heavy hitters with bats finely tuned to the long ball currents at Coors Field in Denver.

This time Nomo had nothing. In his worst outing of the early season, the Rockies pounded Nomo for seven runs and nine hits (including three home runs) in 4⅔ innings, although the Dodgers won the battle of long ball by a score of 12–10. Nomo fell behind 4–0 in the second inning. The Dodgers rallied to take a 6–5 lead into the sixth, but Nomo was unable to hold it. Larry Walker opened the bottom of the sixth with a home run. Two batters later, Dante Bichette leveled a shot into the bleachers for yet another homer. When Nomo surrendered a double just one out later, he was off to the showers.

Nomo left the game in the fifth inning with a 7–6 lead. He made no excuses. "It doesn't matter where I pitch," he stated to those who might find fault with the thin Colorado air. "I don't want to make any excuses. I couldn't make my pitches where I wanted to. I tried to keep the ball low. [But] when the team wins, I'm happy. I want to let people know that I can compete at this level."

Catcher Mike Piazza showed a little more sympathy and understanding. "It's not an easy park to pitch in for anyone," said the Dodgers All Star catcher. "[Nomo] is going to be okay—as long as somebody lets him know not every park is like this one."

Yet the jury was still out. Nomo had started two games, and was the pitcher of record in neither.

His earned run average was a hefty 6.52, hardly the stuff from which legends are built. He had pitched 9⅔ innings, walking six and striking out 14. Both had been road starts. Now it was off to Los Angeles to make his Dodger Stadium debut against the St. Louis Cardinals on May 12.

Nomo's L.A. debut was big-time drama. An ad appeared in the *Los Angeles Times*, which also included such frills as player autograph sessions to encourage ticket sales:

"The Tornado Sweeps into Dodger Stadium: Hideo Nomo Makes Dodger Stadium Debut Tonight. Hideo Nomo is nicknamed 'The Tornado,' because of his unique windup and delivery. Nomo led Japan's Pacific League in wins and strikeouts four of the past years. [So] make your ticket plans now for this historic event."

There was a strong Japanese contingent at the game. Of the 150 media credentials the Dodgers issued, eighty-five were to the Japanese media, who were treated to sushi before the game. There were salvos of cheers and applause as Nomo took to the mound. Flashbulbs were flickering everywhere, as thousands of fans wanted to photograph Nomo and his trademark windup.

With a crowd of 34,159 on hand, Nomo seemed nervous. His first warm-up pitch sailed high over the left shoulder of catcher Carlos Hernandez. He did not get off to a good start either. The Cardinals scored two first-inning runs without the benefit of a hit.

Nomo walked leadoff hitter Bernard Gilkey to start the game, but the Cardinal left-fielder was cut down stealing. Then after two were gone, Nomo found himself in trouble again. Ray Lankford reached first on an Eric Karros error. Nomo walked Todd Zeile and third baseman Scott Cooper to load the bases. Brian Jordan tapped a routine grounder that Dodger third baseman Garey Ingram booted for an error. Lankford and Zeile both came in to score.

The Dodgers took a 3–2 lead into the third inning, but Nomo walked the Cards' Danny Scheaffer on a full count to force in the tying run. With the score tied at three apiece, Nomo gave way to a pinch-hitter. In the sixth inning the Dodgers broke the game open, as Raul Mondesi hit a two-run shot into the left-field bullpen to give Mondesi three RBIs on the day. The Dodgers went on to win by a score of 8–4. Once again Nomo was not the pitcher of record.

It was a mixed bag. While he walked seven, he did not yield a hit in his four innings of work. He gave up three runs and struck out five. However,

Gordon Verrell noted in a *Sporting News* sidebar that there were actually more fans in Dodger Stadium when he *didn't* pitch than when he did. The next night the Dodgers would attract a Saturday crowd of 37,188.

What Nomo's first three starts showed was that when he was on target, his vexing mixture of fastballs and forkballs could be devastating. But his work had been inconsistent. In 13⅔ innings he had given up 8 earned runs and 10 hits. He had walked 13 and struck out 19.

On May 17, against the Pittsburgh Pirates he finally showed the baseball world how devastating he could be when his talent came together. It was his second start before hometown fans. Nomo simply sizzled. He was nothing short of sensational. He struck out nine of the first 12 Pirate batters. In seven shutout innings he allowed only two hits, striking out 14 and walking three. The 14 strikeouts were the most by a pitcher to date, and the most strikeouts by a Dodger rookie since Karl Spooner in a Brooklyn uniform fanned 15 New York Giants in 1954.

Nomo left the game with a 2–0 lead in the eighth inning, receiving two standing ovations after delivering key strikeouts. But the Dodger relief corps could not hold the lead, and the Dodgers fell to the Pirates by a score of 3–2. "I think he's earned everyone's respect around here," said veteran knuckleball pitcher Tom Candiotti.

With each new start Hideo Nomo was making new converts. Wherever he pitched, there was a local contingent of Japanese fans, who waved flags and raised placards with K's displayed in boldface letters. Inspired chants of "No-mo, No-mo," came from the cheering throngs. It was as intense as the "Fernandomania" that had swept Dodger Stadium fourteen years earlier.

Mexican-born Fernando Valenzuela knew only slightly more English than Hideo Nomo when he broke into the Dodger camp in 1981. In fact, Fernando—now a fifteen-year veteran—was among Nomo's earliest boosters. "It's good for him to be that way now," said Valenzuela, now with the San Diego Padres. "It allows him to concentrate on his pitching. I know that he's got a lot of press that's watching him, but the only thing he has to do is keep pitching, and don't let the press and pressure get to him."

Even before Nomo, even before Fernando, Chicago White Sox shortstop Chico Carrasquel came to the big leagues in 1950 speaking no English. Carrasquel, who hailed from Venezuela, became the first Latin to start an All-Star Game in 1951. He had the help of relief pitcher Luis Aloma when it came to the English language. "Luis Aloma was my unofficial interpreter, as well as being one of the best relief pitchers in baseball," says Carrasquel, a five-time All-Star shortstop who today announces Spanish language broadcasts for the Chicago White Sox.

According to Tommy Lasorda, who saw the frenzy associated with both Valenzuela and Nomo, Nomomania dwarfed the rampant Fernandomania of fifteen years ago. "It's worse. It's really worse, believe me," Lasorda told the *L.A. Times*. "I came out to the ballpark at one-thirty today, and there were fifteen guys with cameras waiting on him. They want to know everything he eats. They're watching every move he makes."

The Big Apple was the next stop, and the city of New York was quick to embrace Nomo. He declined an invitation to dine at a nearby Japanese restaurant, however, explaining through his interpreter that because he was pitching the next day he was staying in for the night. Ducking autograph-seeking mobs, his only sights of New York City that first night were the hotel escalator, the lobby, the elevator, and ESPN. He then let the honking horns and sirens from the street below lull him to sleep.

New York Mets third baseman Bobby Bonilla was awaiting his chance to hit against Nomo. "I'm really excited to face him," said the Met slugger. Bonilla had grown up in the Bronx, and well remembered his boyhood days. In 1981 he sat in Shea Stadium watching another Dodger rookie pitcher from another land by the name of Fernando Valenzuela help to soothe a strike-torn game. "I was in the upper deck, in the buck-fifty seats, which no longer exist," Bonilla mentioned just hours before he doubled home one of the Mets four runs against Nomo.

Nomo's devoted Asian following was constantly growing. Before the game Japanese-American fans were among the first to appear at Shea Stadium. They waited above the dugout for Nomo to appear. People were calling his name and waving signs when he first made an appearance on the field. Young girls swooned.

The Mets and Dodgers had identical 10–14 records going into the day. Nomo had lowered his earned run average significantly to a respectable 3.48. At first he was as sharp as a samurai sword, striking out four of the first seven Mets. He was shelled for three runs in the bottom of the third, but he settled down and turned in six strong innings. He allowed eight hits and four runs (three earned), while striking out seven. However, this time Nomo took a backseat to Dodger reliever Todd Worrell, whose fine relief work secured a 6–4 Dodger win.

The Dodgers forged ahead with a pair of runs in the eighth. In the bottom of the inning Worrell entered the game after the Mets had loaded the bases. Worrell promptly set the Mets down one, two, three. But it was yet another no-decision for Nomo. As such he entered the record book. According to the Elias Sports Bureau, Nomo became the first pitcher to have five no-decision outings in his first five starts.

Still, there was rampant Nomomania at Shea Stadium that night, as Japanese fans brought their flags and their Dr. K banners. A paid crowd of 19,107 wooped it up after each Nomo strikeout. So many folks were cheering Nomo on that some Mets fans began breaking into "U.S.A." chants, as if they were at the Olympics.

Nomo's string of no-decisions came to an end on May 27, but it was on the losing side. The Montreal Expos beat the Dodgers 5–1, handing Nomo his first loss, and the only time all season he would have a losing record. The sportswriters came down hard on Lasorda. It was suggested that perhaps he had decided to stay with Nomo too long. Whether it was his zeal to garner Nomo his first win, or he was just leery of his inexperienced and faltering bullpen, Nomo simply fell short.

He struggled through the fifth inning, with three walks, two balks, and a run-scoring double to Moises Alou. "I figured he could go out and hold them for an inning or two more," Lasorda said after the game.

Nomo had thrown 110 pitches through the first six innings, and the gamble backfired big-time. He surrendered a leadoff single to Tony Tarasco to open the seventh. He walked Wil Cordero (his seventh pass of the day). After Moises Alou lined a shot to Billy Ashley in left, Lasorda had seen enough and replaced Nomo with left-hander Joey Eischen. When Eischen walked Henry Rodriguez, he in turn was replaced by rookie right-hander Felix Rodriguez. He promptly served up a grand-slam homer to Rondell White—a shot that sailed halfway into the left-field bleachers. In 6⅓ innings Nomo allowed four hits, three earned runs, walking four and striking out nine.

"Today was no good," said a disappointed Nomo after the game. "I had bad control from the first inning on."

It had been an interesting and puzzling month of May. He had pitched 33 innings, allowed 26 hits, and had walked 25. But he had still struck out an impressive total of 49 batters. And while his work might not have been all he had hoped, he had still pitched some excellent baseball. He had caught the media's eye. Both the *Sporting News* and *Sports Illustrated* ran feature stories on him during May. Nomomania was alive and well, and a portent of things to come.

With the soreness of an eight-month baseball strike still permeating the air, a drop in attendance of almost 25 percent from 1994, and a Harris Poll that indicated the game had lost 30 percent of its fans, compounded further by poor television ratings and the apparent demise of the Baseball Network, it was clear that something was very wrong. Looming ahead was an extremely low vote count for the impending All-Star Game, even with fans being able to vote by Internet or toll-free phone calls.

The game needed an invigorating tonic to make things right. A "tornado" was seen charging in the right direction, and it would soon hit hard. The month of June would be the month of Hideo Nomo.

# 7

# The Tornado Strikes

It was just a marvelous month, pure and simple. One would have to look way back into the record book to see anything similar, perhaps back to Bob Gibson's super summer of 1968. Nomo was dominating to the extreme. His right arm was as hot as the southern California sun and his pitches as stupefying as the Los Angeles smog. Perfect is an absolute, so they say. But in the month of June, Hideo Nomo was about as close to perfect as possible, and he had the baseball world whistling a new and happy tune.

On June 2, Nomo made his second start against the New York Mets. These same Mets who had scored four runs on him on May 23 barely touched Nomo this time around. The Dodgers entered the game with a record of 16–19, three games behind the division-leading Giants. But on June 2, it was all Hideo Nomo. A paid crowd of 31,002 gathered at Dodger Stadium to see the Dodgers beat the Mets 2–1. Nomo was brilliant, allowing the Mets just two hits in eight innings to gain his first win.

"He was outstanding," said catcher Bob Prince, who was behind the plate that day. "He moved the ball around, and his forkball was working. . . . I'm sure his first victory was in the back of his mind. He has pitched great this season; it's not like he's been out of any game. But I'm sure this was special for him."

It was clearly a time for cheer and celebration, as Nomo carried a deserved bottle of champagne into the clubhouse after the game. Both of the hits he had allowed were by Bobby Bonilla: a leadoff homer and a sixth-inning single. Nomo added six strikeouts to up his league-leading total to 54, before being replaced by Todd Worrell with one out in the ninth.

A torrent of boos followed pitching coach Dave Wallace when he took Nomo from the game following a walk to Rico Brogna to open the ninth. The enthusiasm was such that Japanese flags were waving in the air throughout the game. Dodger fans stood and cheered in the seventh inning when

Nomo grounded out, after striking out his first two times at bat. At the end of the game when the crowd began chanting for Nomo, he obliged by coming out of the dugout to tip his cap.

It was also a good day for first baseman Eric Karros, who presented Nomo with the ball after the game—a gesture that delighted Nomo to no end. Karros drilled his ninth home run of the season off Bret Saberhagen in the sixth inning to break a 1–1 tie and give Nomo his first victory. It was a special moment for Karros as well. "I'm looking forward to some Japanese commercials, probably tomorrow," he joked. "It was good for Nomo to pitch like that and to get his first victory."

Someone who was not so cordial was losing pitcher Bret Saberhagen. "Funky," Saberhagen said when asked to describe Nomo. "His fastball is average at best, he has a good forkball. I think more than anything, you beat yourself more than he beats you when you face him. He has become a folk hero, that's for sure."

Yes, Hideo Nomo had become a folk hero. But it was just the start. What loomed ahead was the unfolding of a genuine human-interest story that captivated two continents. Hideo Nomo was on a roll. With the increasing pomp and circumstance, crowds both at home and on the road became usually larger than the day before and the day after he pitched. T-shirts with Nomo's name and jersey no. 16 were becoming more increasingly visible. In many parks there were "K" corners in the upper deck, the way there had been for Dwight Gooden when he captivated the country as a strikeout artist his first few years with the Mets.

Nomo had become a huge celebrity in Japan as well. Arkira Matsuo, president of the Mainichi Newspapers, travels back and forth to Japan regularly. "When [Nomo] first left Japanese baseball, there were some who felt that it was not a good thing to leave the organization," Matsuo says. "But now he is a national hero in Japan. Maybe the number one famous person. Even in Japan, Nomo T-shirts are very valuable items. He's a very brave Oriental. I think that is one of the reasons he's popular in America. Nomo is unique as a person. He has contributed to a good feeling between Japan and America. He's been a bridge between two countries and cultures."

On June 7, Nomo turned the tables on the Montreal Expos, the same team that handed him his only loss. As he limited Montreal to six hits in eight innings, the Dodgers trounced the Expos 7–1 to give Tommy Lasorda his 1,500th win as a manager. Nomo's only trouble came early in the first inning, when a single and two walks loaded the bases. Then he bore down. Rondell White fanned for the first out. Nomo forced Scott Fletcher to pop out for out number two. Third baseman Sean Berry was next. He worked Nomo to a 3–1 count, but Nomo threw a perfect strike on the outside corner for a full count. Berry fouled off the next three pitches, before popping out in foul territory to end the inning. Nomo was never in serious trouble again.

His teammates staked him to a 2–0 lead in the bottom of the first. Jose Offerman doubled with one out, and Raul Mondesi followed with his 10th home run of the year. Tim Wallach brought home a pair with a two-run double in the fourth. Delino DeShields and Offerman each had RBI singles during a three-run sixth to send Jeff Fassero, the Expos' seven-game winner, to the showers.

But as Al Jolson used to say, "You ain't seen nothing yet!" On the night of June 14, the Dodgers rode into Pittsburgh in third place with a record of 22–23—4½ games behind the front-running Colorado Rockies. The Dodgers needed a shot in the arm, and Nomo supplied it in a splendid fashion.

No longer a novelty because of his Japanese birth, Nomo totally mesmerized the Bucs and the 10,313 fans who paid their way into Three Rivers

Stadium. He was awesome, striking out 16 as the Dodgers downed the Pirates by a score of 8–5.

Nomo's 16 strikeouts were a high for the year, and eclipsed Karl Spooner's rookie record of 15. His 16 K's were also just two short of the rookie record of 18 set by Montreal's Bill Gullickson in 1980.

Nomo sure had the Pirates' number. A hex might be a more appropriate description. In two consecutive starts he fanned 30 Pirate batters in the fifteen innings he worked. He made a firm believer of Pittsburgh manager Jim Leyland. "For four or five innings there, [Nomo] was pretty much unhittable," Leyland said. "He can throw hard, and that forkball of his is downright nasty."

Jay Bell, Al Martin, and Mark Johnson each struck out three times that night. "I'd rather face Randy Johnson than Nomo, and I've never even faced Johnson before," said Martin, the Pirate left-fielder. "So that tells you what I think of Nomo. Everything he does makes you look real ugly."

Pirate shortstop Jay Bell was asked if Nomo reminded him of anyone. Bell, who had struck out six times in seven at-bats against Nomo, paused and finally came up with a name. "Yeah," he said, "Cy Young!"

What was most satisfying is that Nomo had

defied conventional logic. It had been assumed that Nomo would be easier to hit the second time around. According to Bell, this was a mistaken assumption. He had some advice for the press and would-be doubters.

"If I were you guys," he said, "I'd write about the quality of his pitching and not his delivery. He's a good pitcher because he's got good stuff, not because he has some trick. I heard people say that his delivery is deceiving, but basically all he does is start, stop, and start again. You can't make any excuses."

Nomo walked only two batters. Pirate catcher Mark Parent felt that the Pirate scouting reports made too much of Nomo's control. "We kept hearing how he's wild," Parent said. "What, because he hits a batter once in a while? Come on, this guy paints the corners as good as anyone in the game. And his forkball is the best in the game. This guy is *good*. I mean, *real good*."

Backed by Mike Piazza's two home runs, Nomo built a 5–0 lead into the eighth inning. The Pirates touched him for three hits to open the eighth, and before long they managed to close the score to 5–3. Even with one out and runners on first and second, Lasorda decided to go with Nomo a little further.

Nomo bore down and gave it his gritty best.

Going for his strikeout pitch, he fanned left-handed-hitting Orlando Merced for out number two. Mark Johnson then went down on strikes for Nomo's record-breaking 16th strikeout. Nomo had left the game by the time Pittsburgh's Dave Clark hit a two-run ninth-inning home run off reliever Greg Hansell.

"He was still throwing the ball very well," said Lasorda. "Besides, the way this guy gets out of jams, he reminds me of Doc Gooden a lot." The small but enthusiastic contingent of Japanese fans chanted, "No-mo, No-mo, No-mo," as he struck out the side four times. His strikeout total was flashed with K cards by his Pittsburgh well-wishers.

Nomo was asked whether he was aware of his rookie record 16 strikeouts. Did he have any idea that he was just two shy of Sandy Koufax's all-time franchise record of 18 (Nomo's one-game high in Japan was 17)? Nomo insisted that he wasn't concerned about records, and that he didn't even know who Sandy Koufax was. "Fernando Valenzuela, I know who he is!" was Nomo's reply. Mike Piazza probably summed things up best. "You know something, he doesn't even know who he's facing. But I guarantee everyone knows who he is now."

Tommy Lasorda had seen some of the game's

great strikeout artists, including Koufax and Drysdale. But he insisted he had never seen a pitcher dominate a team like Nomo dominated the Pirates. "What an exhibition you saw," an excited Lasorda said. "He was amazing. He was awesome. You're starting to see the real Nomo."

The second time around—against the Mets, the Expos, and the Pirates—Nomo posted a 3–0 mark. In 24 innings he allowed just 14 hits and struck out 30. His earned run average over these three games was a stingy 1.50.

Against the St. Louis Cardinals on June 19, Nomo was once more on target. He was coasting to his fourth straight win, but watched as his first complete game slipped out of his grasp in the ninth inning. Nomo went a strong 8⅓ innings, allowing the Cardinals just three hits and striking out eight as the Dodgers won by a score of 5–2.

On June 24 he was dazzling again. There was sheer bedlam at Dodger Stadium when Nomo slammed the door on the San Francisco Giants with a two-hit 7–0 shutout performance. The packed house of 53,551—the largest home crowd of the year—cheered wildly through each of Nomo's thirteen strikeouts, erupting into a tumultuous roar each of the four times he retired Barry Bonds, especially when he fanned Bonds in the ninth inning. As he walked off the mound in the seventh and eighth innings, he was greeted with a standing ovation both times. Hideo Nomo was more than a folk hero now. In Los Angeles he had become a cult figure.

"Los Angeles is madly in love with Hideo Nomo," wrote Bob Nightengale in the *Los Angeles Times* on June 25. It certainly seemed that way. The fans screamed and howled as Eric Karros caught pinch-hitter Rikkert Faneyte's pop-up in foul territory to end the game. Immediately, the Dodgers poured out of the dugout to mob Nomo. Manager Lasorda wrapped him with a huge bear hug. Pitching coach Dave Wallace kept slapping his rookie right-hander on the back. Once more the crowd refused to leave until Nomo tipped his cap, a reminder of a baseball era long gone.

Dodger president Peter O'Malley could hardly contain himself either. After the game he phoned downstairs to have Nomo autograph the lineup sheet. Nomo memorabilia was in huge demand. Dodger stores featured everything from Nomo T-shirts to Nomo hats to Nomo balls. A Japanese restaurant was opened in his honor at Dodger Stadium. When asked about the impending All-Star Game, Montreal Expo manager Felipe Alou said without any reservation that if he were naming the squad that day, Nomo would be on it.

But Nomo was not thinking All-Star Game yet.

"It would be a great honor," he acknowledged, "but right now I'm not going to think about it. I just want to help the team. I'm really glad to have the complete game more than a shutout, just because I finally didn't have to leave the mound. The fans were great all night long. It reminded me of my first year with the Kintetsu."

And what a magnificent job of pitching. He was beautiful to watch. "He's not some gimmick or trick the Dodgers are trying to pull over on you," Dusty Baker insisted. "He's the real thing. The guy comes across just as advertised, a strikeout pitcher. I don't care if you come from Ethiopia or Japan, if you're a strikeout pitcher over there, you're going to be a strikeout pitcher over here."

At one time Nomo retired 23 straight San Francisco batters. His 37 strikeouts in his last three games were the most since Sandy Koufax fanned 38 from September 25 to October 2, 1965. His 11.6 strikeouts per nine innings pitched placed him ahead of Nolan Ryan's 1987 record of 11.48.

Perhaps Nomo would have preferred less attention, less of a public fuss, less media hype. But that could never be. The plain truth is that from the start, he could never have been just another Dodger player. Japanese and all Pacific Islanders needed a hero, and here he was. The superb

June only increased the allure. Japanese Americans were proud, and the baseball world at large was fascinated.

On June 29, when Nomo made his second start against the heavy-hitting Colorado Rockies, the crowd began chanting his name even before the national anthem. That night he pitched the Dodgers into first place with a 3–0 shutout. The sights and sounds of Hideo Nomo were everywhere. The playing field and the Dodger clubhouse were jam packed with reporters, and the loyal faithful unfurled Japanese flags. A quartet of teenage girls were wearing Nomo T-shirts. Three middle-aged Japanese men walked out of the Dodger gift shop with almost $600 in Nomo memorabilia.

The Dodgers issued 131 media credentials for the game, including 75 for Japanese reporters and cameramen. According to a team spokesman, it was the largest number of media credentials ever provided to a regular season game at Dodger Stadium. Nomo's $2 million signing bonus hardly seemed significant anymore. The Dodgers had nearly cleared that number in Nomo ticket sales and memorabilia alone. Nomo was baseball's new poster boy. On a given day he could steal the thunder from the Simpson trial in Los Angeles.

Nomo fever had hit Los Angeles, and had hit it big-time.

Nomo memorabilia was providing all kinds of revenue. There was a rush order on all things endorsed by Nomo, and the Dodger gift shop bustled with business. Nomo T-shirts were going for $25; Nomo baseballs for $10; Nomo sweatshirts for $50; Nomo pennants for $5; and Nomo pins for $3. A limited edition of Nomo baseballs went for $15.

Dodger broadcaster Jaime Jarrin had seen it before, but never quite like this. He was stunned. "I never thought I'd see anything like Fernandomania again," said Jarrin, who was also Valenzuela's interpreter. "But it's coming. Believe me, it is coming. This night is the closest thing I've seen to Fernandomania, and it's bringing back very sweet memories. In 1981 Fernando was striking out everybody, and Nomo is striking everybody out [now]." All blinders were lifted. The night of June 29, 1995, Hideo Nomo emerged as one of the three most dominant pitchers in baseball, along with Greg Maddux and Randy Johnson.

Six weeks earlier the Rockies had socked Nomo for nine hits, three homers, and seven runs in 4⅔ innings. This time Nomo stifled the Rockies on six hits while striking out 13. Six different times he struck out two batters in one inning. The heart of the Rockies order—Joe Girardi, Larry Walker, Andres Galarraga, and Dante Bichette—went 1 for 14 against him, striking out six times. His only trouble spot was the eighth inning, when he walked the bases loaded with no outs. Again, as he had done many times before, he pitched himself out of the jam. He got Andres Galarraga on a snappy 1-2-3 double play, and Dodger Stadium lit up in a frenzy of excitement. And when Dante Bichette lined to Jose Offerman to end the inning, the ovation continued to resonate in the ball park.

"There's not many pitchers who can do what he does," said a frustrated Andres Galarraga, who fanned twice that night. "You think it's a forkball and it's a fastball. Then you think it's a fastball and it's a forkball. You just can't recognize it." When Nomo struck out Walt Weiss to end the game, he had set still another record. It was his 50th strikeout in four consecutive starts, a new Dodger record, passing Sandy Koufax, who collected 39 strikeouts in a four-game stretch three different times, the last being August 1, 5, 10, and 14, 1965.

By blanking the Rockies for his second straight shutout, Nomo earned his sixth straight win, and became the first rookie to win six games in a single month without a loss since Tom Browning in 1985 and Mark Fidrych in 1976. During that span his earned run average was a miniscule 0.89. He was named National League Player of the Month for June. He had become the "Toast of the Town," in the City of Angels.

Tommy Lasorda was at a loss for words. He had never seen anything quite like this during his long career. "The guy's amazing, he's awesome," Lasorda said, pausing only to find even more superlatives. "There's no question he should be part of the National League All-Star team. He deserves it. He earned it." Yes, he did. And earlier that day Felipe Alou had determined the same thing too. Hideo Nomo from Osaka, Japan, would be named to the National League All-Star squad.

The All-Star Game was still two weeks away, but Nomo's exploits had hardly gone unnoticed in the American League. "I think he's been tremendous for baseball," said Detroit Tiger general manager Joe Klein. "Obviously his timing couldn't have been better. Both leagues have taken a blow with [Seattle's] Ken Griffey and [San Francisco's] Matt Williams going down."

Kansas City Royal general manager Herk Robinson added some praise of his own. "I think he's been good for the game. I think he's been one of the bright spots of the season. The Dodgers should be proud of what they have done. I wished we could have signed him."

Sandy Alderson, the Oakland A's general manager noted Nomo's impact on the game in general and the 1995 season in particular. "Nomo has been critical to keeping interest in baseball at the level it is. It transcended the situation in L.A. I think it goes beyond the fact that he's Japanese. It has to do with his ability, which certainly is great. But I think it really has to do with his style. His body language, his manner overall. He's self-effacing and the antithesis of what people have come to expect from baseball players."

The Nomo express still had one more stop before the All-Star break. On July 5, the Dodgers and Nomo took on the Atlanta Braves. A partisan Atlanta crowd of 36,922 watched as Nomo and Atlanta's John Smoltz engaged in one of the finest pitching duels of the season. "It was almost like I was wishing that Nomo and John could have thrown 18 innings apiece," said Brave third baseman and rookie of the year candidate Chipper Jones, whose ninth-inning three-run, two-out, game-winning homer off Dodger reliever Rudy Seañez lifted the Braves to a 4–1 victory. "It was fun. A pitcher as unique as Nomo doesn't come along every day."

"Nomo Is Again Dazzling, But Braves Win in Ninth," wrote the *New York Times* on July 6, 1995. "The matchup was promising: Hideo Nomo, the Los Angeles Dodgers' rookie sensation, against the Braves' John Smoltz. But the result was even better than advertised."

An exquisite pitching duel, most certainly. In seven innings Nomo allowed two hits, one run, walked five, and struck out ten. Smoltz was every bit his equal. In eight innings of work, the Atlanta right-hander gave up one run on nine hits, walking three and striking out 12. Moreover, Smoltz was well aware of Nomo's powerful pitching presence. "It would have been very easy to come here tonight and not know who was pitching for the Braves," said Smoltz, who carried a 7–4, 2.84 ERA into the contest. "I think a lot of people came out tonight just to see how Nomo would pitch. It wasn't so much that I was trying to have more strikeouts, or outpitch him, but I wanted to let people know there was another pitcher in this game."

This was only the second time that the opposing pitcher had recorded more strikeouts than Nomo. He had shut the door on Colorado's big power boys the week before, and this time he did the same with the powerful middle of the Braves batting order. Chipper Jones, Fred McGriff, David

Justice, and Ryan Klesko struck out six times, and hit only two balls out of the infield in 14 at-bats among them.

Through the first week of July, Nomo's 119 strikeouts led all National League pitchers. He lowered his ERA to a nifty 1.99, and had allowed just 4.89 base hits per nine innings pitched, which was almost two hits less than three-time Cy Young winner Greg Maddux. Nomo was a bit miffed by his lack of control against the Braves. He allowed five walks, including two in the first inning when Marquis Grissom scored on a wild pitch. "I got to be better," said Nomo. "Tonight my control was pretty bad."

But the Braves were convinced. Chipper Jones couldn't praise Nomo enough. "I know a lot of people are talking about me as the rookie of the year, but after what he's done all month, even I consider Nomo the rookie of the year. . . . The guy was absolutely phenomenal. He's worth all the press and hype that he's getting. . . . we breathed a sigh of relief when he left the game. It pumped us all up."

If praise from one's peers means anything, maybe Smoltz himself said it best. "Guys were coming back to the bench telling each other that if you let him, he will walk you nine out of ten times.

But they still couldn't lay off his pitches. *He's that good!"*

Hideo Nomo lit up the baseball world in June. There was no brighter star in the game. He had crossed the proverbial Rubicon and established himself as a pitcher of the first rank. He had captured the baseball hearts of two nations, and soothed a game sorely in need. It was a happening whose time had come, and it was called Nomo Mania.

# 8

# Nomomania

"**M**y God, it's unbelievable how many cameras show up for this guy," said Tommy Lasorda after the All-Star Game. "He's the real thing too. He has great talent on the mound, and he's a good guy."

No question that Nomomania had become contagious. John Schuerholz, executive vice president of the Atlanta Braves, was caught in the frenzy as well. He left his office in Fulton-County Stadium early on July 5 to join the festivities on the field. What Schuerholz encountered was unlike anything he had yet to see. The scenario was that of a playoff game or a World Series. More than 100 reporters, minicams, photographers, microphones, and every other piece of electronic equipment pervaded the Dodger dugout. There was even a reporter from a local newspaper covering the Japanese journalists who were covering Nomo.

"This is something else," Schuerholz said. "I usually don't come on the field like this, but I wanted to witness it for myself." Once more he told the press that Nomo could have played for the Braves had he wanted, that he had been scheduled to fly to Atlanta to visit in February but had called to cancel. "We had some serious interest, but it didn't work out," he repeated. "I don't know whether we could have given him a $2 million-plus package, but we had scouts over in Japan who said we should sign him. We were well aware of his ability."

This poses an interesting question. Could Nomomania have taken such hold in Atlanta, considering that there are only 5,000 Japanese living in Georgia, or some other part of the country with a small Japanese population? Scheurholz acknowledged that there was a unique situation considering the large Asian population in southern California, but he left no doubt that had Nomo pitched the way he had with the Dodgers, he would be just as big in Atlanta.

Certainly, Nomo's presence transcended the city of Los Angeles and greatly impacted on the popularity of the game. A look at the attendance figures as of July 4, 1995, indicates this. Through the first 33 games of the season, the Dodgers drew 1,284,165 fans. Only the Colorado Rockies in the National League had drawn more. And among all clubs just the Rockies and the Baltimore Orioles—with Cal Ripken's consecutive-game record in the making—drew more paying customers. Driven by the Nomomania factor, moreover, the average Dodger per-game attendance was above most teams. Dodger attendance averaged 37,056, far better than the National League average of 24,696, and better still than the major league average of 24,343.

It is Mike Downey of the *Los Angeles Times* who takes credit for coining the term Nomomania. "After the first major league baseball game pitched by the Occidental tourist, Hideo Nomo—a real thing of beauty at a real thing of ugly, Candlestick Park in San Francisco—I was so impressed that my entire first paragraph on the next day's *Times* sport pages read: 'Nomomania!' "

After Nomomania had been picked up by ESPN, CNN, KABC, radio talk-show hosts, and fans in the stands, a T-shirt company called Downey to ask if he had copyrighted the term. Then a Tokyo television station asked him to tape an interview explaining how and why he had coined the term and when he first used it.

"I hemmed a little, then hawed some," Downey said, then ultimately confessed that Fernando Valenzuela, who begat Fernandomania, had been my inspiration upon first encountering Hideo Nomo, who begat Nomomania."

Downey never regretted the start of something big, not for one moment. In his mind Nomo saved baseball. He was the best thing that could have happened to the game. In the crazy world of baseball 1995 style, Hideo Nomo "was precisely the right man at precisely the right time," Downey argues.

How do Fernandomania and Nomomania compare? Fernandomania broke out in 1981 when Valenzuela was just 20 years old, with little professional seasoning. Nomo, by contrast, was 26, with five seasons as a Japanese professional behind him, and he pitched with the poise of a 10-year veteran.

In 1981, Valenzuela's rookie year, the season was split and shortened to 110 games because of a strike. Similarly, in 1995, when Nomo came on the scene, an incredibly bitter strike had canceled the World Series for the first time in 90 years, and had deprived tens of millions of fans a chance to see several hallowed records challenged: most visibly

Hideo Nomo greets the press. *(Hokubei Mainichi)*

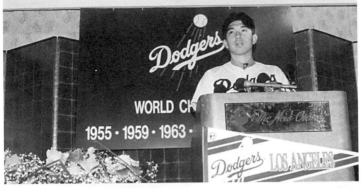

ANGELES DODGERS WELCOME HIDEO N
茂英雄 ドジャース 入団発表記者会

The Dodgers welcome Nomo to America on February 13, 1995,
after he signed a minor league contract with the club.
*(AP/World Wide Photos)*

Nomo is all smiles after winning his first major league game by
beating the New York Mets on June 2, 1995, and is congratulated
by Dodger catcher Tom Prince. *(AP/World Wide Photos/
Damian Dovargnes)*

A relaxed Nomo enjoys a workout with one of his Dodger teammates. *(Hokubei Mainichi)*

In addition to striking out 12 of the hard-hitting Rockies, Nomo helps his team to a 3–0 win over Colorado with a sacrifice bunt. *(AP/World Wide Photos/Chris Martinez)*

These four photos show the trademark windup that baffled major leaguers everywhere. First, shown here in a game against the Pittsburgh Pirates where he strikes out 14, Nomo stretches his arms over his head...

...then, à la former Dodger sensation Fernando Valenzuela, he hurls himself around toward the outfield...

...uncoils, arms
and legs spread
wide...

Tony Inzerillo

...and fires.

Tony Inzerillo

Nomomania seizes Dodger fans as they cheer Nomo on against the arch rival Giants in San Francisco. *(Hokubei Mainichi)*

A Tokyo sports shop manager shows off one of his hottest items on July 11, the day of the All-Star game. Before long, all the memorabilia is sold out. *(AP/World Wide Photos/Itsuo Inouye)*

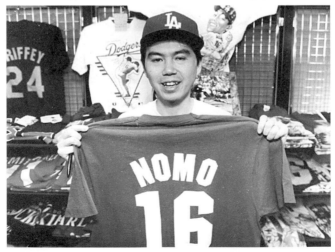

Nomo excitedly awaits his introduction at the All-Star Game at the Ballpark in Arlington, Texas, flanked by fellow all-stars Matt Williams of the San Francisco Giants and Craig Biggio of the Houston Astros. *(AP/World Wide Photos)*

This 1990 photo shows Nomo, then with the Kinetsu Buffaloes, with slugger Kazuhiro Kiyohara, Oakland A's pitcher Dave Stewart, and Detroit's Cecil Fielder, demolishing a sake barrel before an All-Star exhibition series in Japan. *(AP/World Wide Photos/Fujio Yokoyama)*

A crowd gathers in front of Tokyo's Shibuya station to watch
Nomo in his All-Star debut on a giant TV screen.
*(AP/World Wide Photos/Katsuji Kasahara)*

Matt Williams's shot at 61 homers, and a potential .400 season by Tony Gwynn.

Both Nomo and Fernando came to the Dodgers with little English skills but plenty of willingness to succeed. Valenzuela went 13–7 in the shortened 1981 season. Nomo finished the 1995 season with a record of 13–6. Fernando fanned 180 hitters in 192 innings; Nomo set down 236 batters in 191.1 innings. Valenzuela posted a 2.48 ERA in 1981, Nomo a 2.54 ERA in 1995.

In 1981 Valenzuela led the National League in strikeouts, innings pitched, complete games, and shutouts. In 1995 Nomo led the National League in strikeouts, fewest hits per nine innings, and most strikeouts per nine innings, and was second to Greg Maddux in ERA. Valenzuela was both National League Rookie of the Year and Cy Young winner in 1981. Nomo battled the Braves Chipper Jones for Rookie of the Year honors, but with Maddux so dominant in the second half, he was not a viable Cy Young contender—but for that matter, neither was any other National League pitcher.

Nomomania had taken hold on the other side of the Pacific as well. "Interest in major league baseball here used to be limited, said Nobuhisa Ito, an aide to Japan's baseball commissioner. "We have 125 million people in Japan. Now we have 125 million big-league baseball junkies. Everybody is rooting for him." For Nomo's pitching debut against the Giants on May 2, Japanese journalists filed uplifting dispatches that knocked subway gas attacks off the front pages, and newspapers charted the type and result of each of Nomo's 91 pitches.

"We all kind of figured it was going to happen," said former California Angel first baseman Lee Stevens, who spent the 1994 season with Nomo in Japan. "But we were kind of surprised that it actually happened when it did. He had some arm trouble last year and didn't get to do as well as he wanted to."

Nomo's old team, the Kintetsu Buffaloes, was still suffering from his departure. After a second-place tie last season, the Buffaloes were at the bottom of the Pacific League with a 32–46 record at the All-Star break. Nomo's departure from Japanese baseball made some of the other clubs a bit skittish, and was tough on Japanese franchise executives trying to keep other players from following him.

"Until now not many had dreams of playing in the big leagues," said Kioshi Onosaka, public relations director for the Kintetsu Buffaloes. "Amateur players could dream, but once they turned pro in Japan, they stayed here. Dreams of children have expanded twofold because of Nomo's success. Recently in Japan the amount of signing bonuses has increased. Money is important, but the hunger to become a professional is still what drives young players."

In Tokyo and other Japanese cities people would gather on street corners to watch "The Tornado" on giant televisions. Screens were set up in public places, and NHK, the public broadcasting corporation, would broadcast Nomo's games live on one of its satellite channels. Every day TV stations broadcast long reports about Nomo's success, always showing endless clips of American fans chanting, "Nomo, Nomo, Nomo," from the stands.

If television wasn't quite enough for the faithful, Japan Travel Bureau, a large travel agency, offered "Dodger Watching" tours to Los Angeles. These included a round-trip flight, three nights in a hotel, a game at Dodger Stadium (hot dog included), a side trip to Disneyland and other attractions, with prices ranging from $1,250 to $2,700.

Nomo fever hit Japan in a big way. It might not have been time to talk to the Japanese about trade with the United States, or to commemorate the end of World War II, or to discuss the rainy July weather. But any talk about baseball, specifically Hideo Nomo, was open season. He had become a matinee idol in his native country, where a baseball player is like a movie star.

The hottest-selling item in Japan was a Nomo Dodger jersey. He provided Japan with an emotional boost during a difficult year. A credit association in Osaka even raised the interest rate on special saving accounts by 0.001 percent for every Nomo strikeout.

"He's so handsome, don't you think?" said Midori Ashida, a Tokyo scientist, as she admired Nomo's picture on the cover of a national magazine. "He's our best hope." Nomo's nickname, "Tornado," became one of the most popular English phrases in Japan. Japanese who didn't speak much English were happy to use phrases like "Tornado" and "MVP" to convey their hopes for Japan's first major league all-star.

Kaneo Ikeda, a salesman in Japan, claimed to be "psychohappy" about Nomo's baseball exploits. Like many Japanese, he tried to get up at 4:30 A.M. Japanese time to watch Nomo pitch on TV. Japanese columnists found political solace as well, suggesting that the American acceptance of Nomo, and the willingness to name him to the All-Star team, were indications of the openness and fairness of the American system. "We have had some bad times because of the doomsday cult killing twelve people and injuring more than five thousand. But Nomo's brilliance at America's national pastime is making Japanese feel better about themselves," said computer scientist Koichi Okamoto.

In a Major League Baseball Japan shop in Tokyo, customers snapped up Nomo caps, shirts and other merchandise in droves. According to store official Hiaso Kanayama, each time a new shipment of Nomo goods arrived, at least 40 people were outside waiting before the store opened.

According to Masaru Ikei, a political science professor at Tokyo's Keio University who has written two books on baseball, "Nomo is better than a hundred Japanese ambassadors to Washington." He argues that Nomo has also helped break more Japanese stereotypes than he fits. He has been able to impress fans on both sides of the Pacific with his taciturn, get-the-job-done demeanor. It evokes the way Japanese sumo wrestlers handle themselves, attempting to exude a Buddha-like serenity coupled with a humble sense of confidence and strength.

He is very cool with the press, usually giving

them only small comments, Akira Matsuo points out. He has handled the press in a way few Japanese athletes would have. When he isn't ignoring reporters, he answers questions with a brevity and candor rare among Japanese players, most of whom have their eyes on broadcasting careers and product endorsements. Of course, if this was international trade, the United States would be running a surplus with Japan, it can be argued. There have been dozens of exports of American players to Japan over the years.

Nomomania became big business as well, with a few unusual twists and turns. Nike, who aired the two Nomo commercials during the All-Star Game, hoped that the game might become *The Hideo Nomo Show*. "Who cares whether he speaks English?" Nike's Keith Perter was quoted as saying. "He lets his pitching do his talking for him."

In addition to Nike, Nomo has a U.S. endorsement contract with sunglasses maker Killer Loop. In Japan he has deals with Sumitomo Life Insurance Company. Interestingly, however, most large Asian corporations that advertise in the mainstream American market wouldn't turn to Nomo, because they want to appear as American as possible. The same was so while Fernando Valenzuela was the talk of baseball. His Mexican nationality cost him a number of national endorsement contracts.

In the Little Tokyo area of Los Angeles, a string of tourist novelty shops hang signs over the walkway to persuade people passing by that "official" Nomo goods can be found inside. In one of the stores, company president Akira Fujimoto said that about 20,000 T-shirts have been sold at his firm's six local stores this season. Nomo's fame, he said, has brought the Japanese back to an area that has been blighted the last several years with incidents that discouraged visiting.

Nomo certainly has made his mark on Little Tokyo's storefront windows, where Dodger T-shirts emblazoned with no. 16 hang by the scores, with such items as $200 signed baseballs and even an English song on audio cassette called "The Ballad of Hideo Nomo." Sales of T-shirts have flagged slightly because long-sleeved shirts are favored in Japan with the beginning of autumn. The New Otani Hotel in Los Angeles, located in a tree-lined shopping area that feels like a transplanted bit of Japan, has a lounge where Japanese business people gather together regularly to watch Nomo play.

He has also done wonders for the local nightlife. After a Nomo game in Los Angeles, throngs of people head to Little Tokyo. All the restaurants are open until twelve or one o'clock so people can enjoy a good meal. A Japanese radio station is in the making in Los Angeles.

Nomo's performance in the big leagues—and to a lesser extent the strong showing of two Japanese tennis players at Wimbledon—was a welcome relief for a troubled Japan in 1995. "Nomo's impact [in the United States] will be so great as to recast the image of the Japanese people in the American imagination," according to a Washington correspondent for Japan's Mandichi newspapers. Hideo Nomo had become a Japanese hero (the name Nomo actually means hero in Japanese), in large part because he's a genuine individualist who succeeded on his own merits and his own terms in the world of American baseball.

Visitors from Japan will tell you that the best gifts from friends is a Nomo T-shirt. "People save money to buy these T-shirts because they are not sold everywhere in Japan," says Mitsufumi Okabe, president of Japan Television Network, who also heads Pacific Leisure Management, a San Francisco–based company that provides tours, guides, and interpreters for visitors from Japan. More and more Japanese people are traveling to cities in the United States to see baseball, Okabe adds. "More firms are going to bring visitors here, and whole programs are already being worked out and prepared for next year."

Hidemi Kittaka of the Tushin News Service says, "Men like me are so proud of Nomo, and what he's doing for our country. When you talk to women now, they say, 'Oh, I didn't know Nomo was so cute.' It doesn't make you feel too good when your girlfriend is saying that, but because it's Nomo you can understand."

There has been some worry that other players, prompted by Nomo's success, would seek fame and fortune in the United States too. Japanese pitchers are considered the best candidates. "I have thought for years that there are Japanese players, especially pitchers, with the talent to play in the major leagues, but Nomo has opened the door," says Akira Matsuo, publisher and president of the Mainichi Newspapers, certainly no stranger to either Japanese or American baseball.

Former Texas Ranger manager Bobby Valentine, who managed Japan's Chiba Lotte Marines, concurs completely. "The top twenty pitchers here," he insists are all major league standard or above." Valentine feels strongly that the creative minds on both sides of the ocean should sit down immediately and plan a meeting of "dream teams" in

Atlanta for the 1996 Olympics. "They should feed off the interest Nomo has generated to create a real worldwide competition," he says.

Certain Japanese players have stated that they would like to play in the United States. But as we have seen, this could be difficult because Japanese contracts are very strict. Free agency is a new concept in Japan and applies only to veterans of ten years' standing. Moreover, the commissioners of baseball in the United States and Japan have an agreement that controls trans-Pacific raiding. Even when a player retires from Japanese baseball and moves to the United States, he cannot sign with an American club without first getting permission from the player's old Japanese team.

The truth is that Nomo's situation was a rare one. The Kintetsu Buffaloes let him go after his bad season, and his demands for a multiyear contract. Yet realistically they let their prime prospect go without even demanding compensation. So realistically the possibility of a Japanese invasion of American baseball in the 1990s is not likely.

What is interesting is that six months earlier, when Nomo first chose to leave Japanese baseball, many considered him a rebel, a temperamental athlete who "quit" when his team refused his demands for a multiyear contract. Before he left for the United States in January, many in the Japanese media outlets condemned Nomo, and his teammates treated him coolly. Some sportswriters found him uninteresting because he often said so little in response to their questions. Nomo's flight to the United States, some said, would destroy order in Japanese baseball. His salary in Japan of 140 million yen ($1.6 million) was about a third of what Japan's biggest baseball stars were making.

Yet such skepticism was short-lived. By the time the 1995 All-Star Game rolled around, he had become a hero in his native Japan. "The most famous Japanese in America is neither Prime Minister Tomiichi Murayama nor Minister of International Trade and Industry Ryutaro Hashimoto," wrote Yashuhiro Tase in the *Nihon Keizai* newspaper. "It is the pitcher 'Tornado' Nomo, who is building up a mountain of strikeouts with his forkball."

Not only had Nomo become the prototype local boy who made good, and Japan's most prized export, he had also given Japan's image in the United States a human touch. He became a romantic symbol to many, an independent spirit who threw away a safe career to pursue a dream. Even politicians who were campaigning for a parliamentary election in July talked about Nomo. To many

Japanese, Nomo typified someone who wanted to test his ability in an environment of freedom, not found in the strictures and constraints of Japanese corporate culture. In one TV debate, Kenichi Omae, leader of Heisel Group, a fledgling political party, argued that Nomo's refusal to tolerate the conditions of his Japanese team was an example of how voters should act if they wanted to improve their living conditions.

Kelko Kishj, an actress running for a seat in the upper house, said Nomo's attitude gave her a feeling of "refreshment." In fact, Nomo's countrymen became so enamored with his fastballs, forkballs, and strikeouts that a leading Japanese life insurance company signed a contract with him to do commercials for 100 million yen, which translates into 1.1 million American dollars.

"Six months after entering the country, Nomo has become Michael Jackson in a baseball uniform," writes the *Los Angeles Times*'s Bob Nightengale. "The moment he appears on the field, women shriek, men forget their age, children flock toward him. Soon you'll be able to see him in a Japanese-made car commercial, selling life insurance, drinking coffee, and donning sports apparel, when he isn't hawking tennis shoes or sunglasses.

There's even a Nomo calling card offered by a Japanese telephone company."

Dodger broadcaster Vin Scully even got into the act. During games which Nomo started, he would use Japanese phrases. In one game he hastened from his broadcast booth to find Japanese journalists. He had been counting Nomo strikeouts in Japanese, but alas, he could only count as high as six, *roku* in Japanese, when he realized Nomo would strike out more than that. To count up to ten, he quickly scribbled the following: *shichi*, *hachi*, *ku*, *ju* (seven, eight, nine, ten). He worked that out well. But when Nomo struck out his 11th batter, Scully mumbled nervously. "Let's just call it *ju* plus one."

So as the 66th All-Star Game approached, Japanese right-hander Hideo Nomo was the man of the hour on two continents. When Nomo was officially named to the National League squad on July 2, it was anticlimactic in comparison with what he had already done. "He's got to be on the team," joked National League Manager Felipe Alou to the *Dallas Morning News*. "You're talking about a trade war if he isn't on the team."

The editorial lead in the *Dallas Morning News* pleaded for Alou to pick Nomo as the National

League's starting pitcher. Alou, however, made it clear to the media who covered the Montreal Expos that Atlanta's Greg Maddux would start the mid-summer classic. But as public sentiment toward Nomo started to grow, there was a change of heart. Even Maddux himself got into the fray, adding a little levity of his own. "Hey, if I was a fan, I'd rather see Nomo start too," Maddux said. "I'm boring!"

Hardly true, of course. But one thing was very clear. No matter how well Hideo Nomo did in the All-Star Game—or even the remainder of his career, for that matter—he had already etched a mark on baseball that would not be erased. And his place in the history of the Dodger organization in particular had already been firmly established.

# 9

# Starlight in Texas

The *New York Post* headlined its sport pages of July 11, "Stars and Scars." *USA Today Baseball Weekly* captioned its All-Star Game issue, "Lone Stars Call a Truce: But Will Fans Return?" Pete Williams, writing for *Baseball Weekly*, headlined his column, "FanFest Festers Wounds: Prices Add to Baseball's Reputation for Greed."

The implication was clear. Even with all the hype and hoopla to highlight the 66th All-Star Game—including an old-timers' game and a home run hitting contest, won by the White Sox Frank Thomas—baseball was still on the mend. A tarnished game was in trouble, cynicism ruled the airwaves and print media, and the great Mickey

Mantle, in the last stages of a terminal illness, was courageously telling kids, "Don't be like me."

To assuage some of the ill feeling from the long baseball strike, the Fifth Annual "All-Star FanFest" was held July 7-11 at the Dallas Convention Center. Yet many writers and pundits were critical of a celebration that they felt showed more glitter than merit. "What nonsense!" Pete Williams wrote in *Baseball Weekly*. "If FanFest is really an opportunity to generate goodwill toward fans, to mend fences at a time when interest in baseball is at its lowest ebb, then why are fans charged *twelve dollars* just to attend (OK, so kids get in for a mere eight bucks)."

But if the All-Star Game glitz could not hide baseball's many ills, the Lone Star state at least put on a grand production. The emphasis for obvious reasons was on the positive. "This is a great event to get the game of baseball back on track," echoed Texas governor George Bush, Jr., who used to be managing general partner of the Texas Rangers. "It's a peaceful affair in the midst of this so-called war."

That "so-called war" of which Governor Bush spoke began almost a year earlier on August 11, 1994, when the players' union called a strike one month after the 1994 mid-summer classic. At the 65th All-Star Game held at Three Rivers Stadium in Pittsburgh, the scuttlebutt around town was about the possibility of a strike. Players and owners had their respective labor leaders in town, and to show solidarity several All-Stars joined their malcontent brethren to discuss when they should walk.

There were other deep-seated and unresolved problems plaguing baseball. For starters, baseball has been without a commissioner since September 1992, when Fay Vincent was fired. Milwaukee Brewers owner Bud Selig has acted as an interim since then. Moreover, the sport didn't have a national television contract for the following season. ABC and NBC, the one-time telecast partners, said "farewell, adios, and good-bye." They had had enough of a game which simply wasn't working. What was left was a hope and prayer that either Fox, CBS, or cable might pull a bailout.

Enter Hideo Nomo. When Greg Maddux pulled out of the All-Star Game at the last moment because of a groin injury, it paved the way for Nomo as the National League starting pitcher. When questioned by the press as to what would happen if Maddux had shown up, Felipe Alou hemmed a bit and coyly talked his way out of an answer. When he finally determined that Nomo would get the nod, Alou proved every bit the diplomat.

"I think this is a special All-Star Game because of [Nomo]," Alou said. "He's from the Far East. I'm from the Dominican Republic—and I'm the first Latin-born manager to manage in the All-Star Game. I believe that's very good for baseball. [Nomo's] very deserving of the honor. He's one of the big things that has happened to baseball."

And it was a good choice. Even Maddux repeated in his modest way that he thought Nomo was more deserving of the honor. "I think more people want to watch him pitch than me, to be honest. He's unique. There's a certain mystique which I don't have." While Maddux would pull so far ahead of the pack during the second half of the season, enough so to assure a record fourth Cy Young Award, Maddux and Nomo had similar numbers at All-Star break. Maddux brought a record of 8–1, 1.64 ERA, 104⅓ innings pitched, 73 hits, 8 walks, and 86 strikeouts. Nomo was 6–1, 1.99 ERA, 90⅓ innings pitched, 51 hits, 46 walks, and a league-leading 119 strikeouts.

One thing was for sure: Nomo was surrounded by great players: Tony Gwynn of the San Diego Padres was a five-time batting champion hitting .363 at the All-Star break, and well on his way to a sixth batting title. The Giants' Barry Bonds, a three-time NL MVP, and the game's top vote getter, was playing in his fifth All-Star Game. Atlanta Braves first baseman Fred McGriff has been one of the game's premier power hitters for years. Ron Gant of the Cincinnati Reds was baseball's great comeback story, having been released by Atlanta after breaking his leg in a bike accident before last season. The Colorado Rockies' Vinnie Castilla, the seventh Mexican to appear in an All-Star Game, replaced the injured Matt Williams, in this his first season as a full-time third baseman. Other National League starters included Houston's Craig Biggio at second base, outfielder Lenny Dykstra of the Phillies, and Cincinnati Reds shortstop Barry Larkin as a lineup replacement for the injured Ozzie Smith.

There was no doubt, however, that Nomo's presence dominated the scene. He had become the media darling, and rightfully so. Baseball writers worked hard to come up with catchy headlines, such as "NOMO A RISING SUN-SATION," which appeared in the *New York Post* on July 11, with an illustration of Nomo's complete delivery sketched in eleven successive stages.

"He is what is good about baseball right now. That's why people are looking at him right now," said the Cardinals Ozzie Smith after the game. "Baseball needs it," said Dodger teammate and fellow All-Star Todd Worrell, commenting on the boost Nomo had given the game.

Perhaps the best appraisal was given by All-Star catcher and battery mate Mike Piazza. "It's a great story. It's amazing the attention and hype he is getting in Japan. I never thought it was going to get this big. . . . It takes a special kind of guy to deal with all that attention. He's done it extremely well and has had a great attitude about it."

Piazza also talked about Nomo's development to Ron Rains of *Baseball Weekly:* "Being successful in that league [Japan] doesn't translate to success over here. I was pretty skeptical like everyone else. When I caught him early in spring training, I really thought he was going to Triple A.

"Basically, he has been very receptive to any constructive criticism the staff has given him. Over there it is mostly an up-and-down strike zone, and over here it's in and out with the corners. He's learned to pitch on the corners very well. The biggest misconception about him is that he's green and not knowing. He definitely knows how to pitch, and he's got a lot of poise and presence."

About 50 extra Japanese media outlets, double the total that normally covers an All-Star Game, were credentialed for this one. Throngs of photographers surrounded Nomo in the dugout. He had two news conferences at the All-Star workout day, attended by foreign and American journalists, although he spoke through his interpreter and revealed little. One reporter even solicited Nomo's opinion of the other great news story in Los Angeles, the O. J. Simpson trial. Nomo didn't offer any.

But the spotlight was clearly Nomo's. "He's under a microscope," said Mike Piazza. And sometimes the experience got a little extreme. For example, when Nomo was trying to get in his personal workout in the clubhouse—using hand weights while doing arm exercises—a TV cameraman saw him and tried to film him. But Nomo moved behind a wall where he could not be photographed.

Nomo himself seemed calm and unimpressed by the hoopla surrounding the game. After warming up in the bullpen he paused to slap the hands of youngsters leaving the field after the pre-game ceremonies.

Tony Gwynn recalled the All-Star Game and offered some interesting anecdotes. Gwynn speared Cal Ripken's line shot to right field for the final out in the second inning to help Nomo retire the side in order.

"The All-Star Game is the dangest thing I've ever seen. I've never seen anyone follow a guy into the bathroom before," Gwynn said. "Barry Bonds and Ozzie Smith's lockers were right next to me, and Barry looked at me, then looked at Ozzie, and said, 'Damn, man! This is the first All-Star Game where I haven't been the center of attention.' And he was right. Nomo was in a corridor, and there was everybody trying to get to his interpreter. Trying to figure out what he's trying to say. He doesn't say much.

"He was very impressive in the All-Star Game. He made some very professional hitters look like amateurs. Ripken hit a ball real good. Matter of fact, after I caught the ball and came back to the dugout, he bowed to me. I said, 'Hey, don't do that. Just shake my hand.' "

By starting the All-Star Game for the National League, Nomo became only the fourth rookie from either league to do so. The others: Los Angeles' Fernando Valenzuela, Detroit's Mark Fidrych, and Washington's Dave Stenhouse. There seemed to be something for everyone, a bit of the old and the new. Baltimore's Cal Ripken, Jr., was making his 13th-straight All-Star start, and Nolan Ryan, the all-time strikeout king, was throwing out the ceremonial first pitch.

In spite of their mediocre mid-year record of 34–35, the Los Angeles Dodgers were well represented among the National League All-Stars with five players, more than any National League team. Nomo and Mike Piazza drew starting assignments, while outfielder Raul Mondesi, pitcher Todd Worrell, and shortstop Jose Offerman were named to the squad by manager Felipe Alou.

The pitching matchup between Hideo Nomo and Seattle's Randy Johnson was a baseball dream. It featured the strikeout kings from both leagues. "This is the kind of pitching matchup that people want to see," commented Tony Gwynn. "Hopefully it will help get people excited about baseball again." If Nomo provided the game with an international flavor, Randy Johnson, with his height and 97-mph fastball, was high box office appeal. Johnson's numbers certainly warrant mention. Going into the All-Star contest, Johnson led the majors with 152 strikeouts in 109⅓ innings, to go with a 9–1 record and 2.88 ERA.

"He's something different in the game," said Johnson, who at 6'10" is not exactly an average pitcher himself. "When something new happens people want to explore it. The same way when I came up. He's foreign, so that adds to the myth a little more."

Although Nomo seemed unfazed by all the attention being heaped on him, it was obvious that the game meant a great deal to him. "I'm going to play as if my life depends on it," he said through his interpreter. "I wanted to play with the best. When I left Japan to play baseball in the United States, I had some doubts. [But] it has worked out for me okay. I'm up for the challenge. Being picked to be in this game is beyond my wildest expectations."

American League hitters didn't quite know what to expect, not having faced him before. But they were ready for the challenge. "They call it Nomo-mania right now," said New York Yankee third baseman Wade Boggs, appearing in his 11th All-Star Game. "Facing him gives you a little added sensation. It pumps you up a little more."

The Twins' Kirby Puckett, who took that long leap from the Chicago housing projects to become one of baseball's true goodwill ambassadors, was a bit more circumspect. "Good luck to him," said Puckett, playing in his 10th All-Star Game. "I don't change my hitting philosophy for Randy Johnson, so I'm not going to change it for Nomo. I got one theory and one theory only, man: I'm swinging. You can't hit if you don't swing."

If pitching was supposed to carry the night, it certainly did. But more important, the 50,000 plus fans who braved the sizzling heat at Arlington, Texas, saw a darn good ball game.

While pitching ruled much of the game, it was the long ball that eventually put the National League over the top with a 3–2 win, for its 39th All-Star victory in 66 games. Seventeen batters went down on strikes that night in the 96-degree heat. Nomo and Johnson each worked two shutout innings. Each faced six batters and fanned three. Johnson walked one man, and Nomo allowed a first-inning single to Carlos Baerga.

Despite a wave of solid pitching, it was the long ball that made the difference. Four home runs accounted for all five runs, as the Marlins' Jeff Conine provided the margin of victory with a pinch hit homer in the eighth, to put the National League over the top.

The All-Star Game marked the mid-point of the 1995 season. To be a bit more poetic, it was the end of the beginning. For more than a month and a half now, Hideo Nomo had been the talk of the baseball world. His two All-Star Game innings were splendid. Over the past few months "The Tornado" had faced some of baseball's heaviest bats. His All Star outing pitted against such American League sluggers as Frank Thomas and Albert

Belle, and he had closed the door on both. His impact on the game had been nothing less than astounding.

Much had been said of his control, but that issue is deceiving. Giant third-base coach Wendell Kim had been around the league for many years. He had seen pitchers come and go. He found no problem with Nomo.

"Every time I've seen him," Kim explains, "he's always had decent control. He's around the plate, and that's what counts. I think what makes his forkball good are all his other pitches. Maddux has five or six or seven pitches. He takes speed off his change-up, fastball, even his breaking ball. If Nomo only had a fastball and a split, then he wouldn't be that effective. You look at two pitches instead of five. It's a lot easier to pick out fifty percent of the time instead of twenty percent of the time."

Matt Williams sat out the All-Star Game due to injury, but he offers some interesting observations. "I think the key to facing Nomo," he said, "is to make sure the ball is up in the strike zone, and it is a strike. Because if you look at his tapes and watch him pitch, study closely and see how many guys swing at pitches out of the strike zone, whether it's his fastball or a forkball. The number of pitches he throws justifies my statement."

Nomo had been tried and tested. He had shown the mettle from which he was made. Still one doubter was Chicago White Sox first baseman Frank Thomas. "The Big Hurt," who popped out behind the plate in the first inning, was quoted as saying that he didn't find Nomo all that overpowering. He felt that much of the hype centered on the fact that Nomo was the "first" Japanese player to play in the major leagues. "The media is making him into something," Thomas stated. "I don't know if he can keep it up the rest of the season."

Obviously he had never heard of Murakami, but Thomas did bring up a cogent point. For Nomo to remain as mesmerizing as he had been would have demanded the magic of a Merlin. A look at his strikeout ratio per nine innings pitched shows why. He was on a record-shattering pace: better than Nolan Ryan, Dwight Gooden, or Sandy Koufax; better than Herb Score, Bob Feller, or Walter Johnson. In 13 starts for the Dodgers he had struck out 119 batters in just 90⅓ innings, limiting opposing batsmen to a stingy .158 batting average.

*Baseball Weekly* had him running neck and neck with the Atlanta Braves Chipper Jones for National

League Rookie of the Year. Prior to his June surge Nomo had placed a distant third behind Jones and Montreal Expos pitcher Carlos Perez. And Nomo was running second to Greg Maddux, who for the fourth straight year was again putting Cy Young numbers on the register.

"Fans like to see people dominate," Tony Gwynn said before the All-Star Game. "The two guys that are going to throw are the best in baseball as far as dominating hitters. I'm not sure Nomo is the pure power pitcher like Randy Johnson, but I've seen Barry Bonds hit for a few years, and I haven't seen him look as bad as he did against Nomo."

For Hideo Nomo the All-Star Game was an unforgettable thrill. He was one of the first of the players to leave the hotel and arrive at the ballpark. Few people would have faulted him if he had stayed behind for a couple of hours to preserve his strength, considering the sweltering heat. But he didn't delay his arrival a moment.

In the clubhouse, there were accolades and congratulatory notes to wade through. One was a congratulatory fax from Japanese prime minister Tomiichi Murayama. There was a letter from Murhyamama, the grand national sumo wrestling champion. Later he stood on the field giving high-fives to nearly 100 little league players. Nomo loved it. In plain talk, he was having the time of his life.

Chicago Cub relief pitcher Randy Myers admired the way Nomo could relax. "Man, it was a kick being around the guy," Myers said. "You know, he was even lifting weights today before he pitched. He's my kind of guy. When we went on the field today with all those cameramen, I just said, 'Stay close to me, Nomo. I'm your body-guard. You follow me and you'll be all right."

Myers, a martial arts expert, expressed only one regret. "The only thing I was disappointed in was that he didn't go eight [innings]. I know it was against the rules, but hey, that's what everyone wants to see anyway."

Nomo did not feel the intense pressure one might expect. He wanted to do his best. But more than that he just enjoyed the thrill of being there. "It didn't matter if we won or lost, I wanted to enjoy myself. If I gave up some hits, I wasn't going to worry about it. I just wanted to have fun."

That's just what he did. After his two innings of work, Nomo spent the rest of the game enjoying himself on the bench. Unlike other National League players who headed to the clubhouse once they were removed from the game, Nomo was still in the dugout in full uniform, shaking hands with his teammates.

"I was the last one off the field when I walked in from the bullpen," said Dodger closer Todd Worrell. "And there was Nomo with this grin on his face waiting for me. I couldn't believe it. How professional can you get?"

As the 1995 baseball season was about to enter its second half, there had been accolades galore and stories aplenty for Hideo Nomo. There were well-orchestrated soliloquies by the press and the media. Nomo was big-time baseball news. With Cal Ripken's record still pending, Nomo's pitching heroics had become the biggest baseball story of a strike-torn season.

Fred Claire, Dodger executive vice president, perhaps wrapped it up best. His message was sweet, simple, and to the point. "I just have the greatest respect for him," Claire said with utter sincerity.

# 10

# All-Star Aftermath

"**I**n an era of deliveries made efficient to the bone," wrote Dave Kindred in the *Sporting News*, "Nomo is a rococo stylist whose elaborate choreography is a puzzlement that delights." No doubt Nomo had done ordinary work in a most extraordinary way. On five different occasions through early July, Nomo had given up two or fewer hits in seven innings. During a stretch of four games in June and July he had struck out 50 batters, more than Sandy Koufax over a similar stretch. "As unorthodox as [Nomo] is by American standards," Lasorda stated, "he's got great poise. Because as good a pitcher as he is, he is a better person. Right now he is just baffling hitters, and not just bad hitters. He has made some real good hitters look really bad."

For example, in an outing against the Atlanta Braves, Nomo faced big Fred McGriff with the bases loaded and the score tied 0–0. Through a salvo of tomahawk chop chants and other stadium roars, Nomo handcuffed the mighty McGriff, who fouled out weakly. When a Japanese reporter asked McGriff which of Nomo's pitches was better, his fastball or his forkball, McGriff hesitated a few seconds. "The windup," he said with a bit of tongue in cheek.

According to Tom Lasorda and pitching coach Dave Wallace, Nomo's vast improvement came when he learned to bring his pitches down. This is understandable. Akira Matsuo, the president of the Mainichi Newspapers in Northern California, played baseball in Japan himself. Matsuo points out that the strike zone is higher in Japan, and this factor helps explain why Nomo was walking more batters earlier in the year.

Suguru Egawa, a former fastball pitcher for the Yomiuri Giants and now a commentator, offers another interesting point. American baseballs are a millimeter wider than the baseballs in Japan, he maintains, and the bigger ball in America better fits Nomo's hand. Some Japanese have also speculated that Nomo has been helped by a bigger strike zone in America. The area in which umpires will call a strike is reputed to be the equivalent of one and a half baseballs bigger than the Japanese strike zone.

Nomo himself has told Japanese reporters that he feels the American strike zone is bigger. One reason is the positioning of the umpires. Umpires in Japan call their pitches from above the catcher's head. In America the umpires tend to watch the pitches in between the batter's body and the catcher's face.

Nomo had also proven a sound financial investment. Through the long summer months, Nomo meant money in the bank for the Dodger organization. During his first eight home starts, Nomo attracted 328,372 fans to Dodger Stadium, an average of 41,047 per game. This exceeded the season average by nearly 4,000. When all the revenue had been added up—tickets, parking, and concessions—the club generated at least an extra $70,000 each time Nomo took to the mound.

With Nomomania soaring to unprecedented heights, and as attendance approached the 50,000 mark for five straight Nomo outings, the Dodgers netted another million dollars. The stadium gift shop became a veritable cottage for "Nomobilia" of all types. There was Nomo everything: caps, T-shirts, jerseys, pins, pennants, and foam-rubber K's (for his strikeouts). The gift shop hours were extended during home games, and the sudden influx of Asian fans prompted the team to set up a visitors' information booth manned by Japanese-speaking guides.

A Japanese-type restaurant appeared among the concessions. To capitalize on Nomo's enormous popularity, the Dodgers began offering sushi in the stands during home games. Stadium vendors, clad in *happi*, sold 10-piece boxes of sushi for $5.25. Even so, the more traditional choices remained more popular with fans. At least old-line vendor, peanut man Roger Ownes, wanted no part of the hype. "I made my career on peanuts," he said, "and I'm not going to change now."

Despite Nomo's pitching heroics, however, it had been a disappointing first half for the Dodgers. With a lineup including the likes of Eric Karros and Mike Piazza, both of whom would put MVP numbers on the board, second-year outfielder Raul Mondesi, by all standards a superstar in the making, the exquisite pitching of Hideo Nomo, and five members of the National League All-Star squad, the Dodgers were in trouble.

They had been picked as the team to beat in the

preseason, yet the Dodgers entered the second half of the season with a losing record of 34–35, five games behind the front-running Colorado Rockies. So close was the division race, in fact, that the San Diego Padres and the San Francisco Giants were just a game behind the Dodgers.

Reports emanating from the Dodger clubhouse indicated there was grumbling in the ranks. The level of the discontent was growing louder and louder. The Dodger pitching staff was ranked only behind the Atlanta Braves' great staff, but the defense had become porous, perhaps the worst in the league. The Dodger offense, while strong in the middle of the order, had failed in the clutch. If there was an encouraging sign, it was that of the four teams in the National League West, the Dodgers had the most room for improvement.

But some of the troops were clearly unhappy, most specifically second baseman Delino De-Shields. After being benched for four games, his feelings were hurt and he was talking retirement. "I've got my house and car paid for. . . . I might decide I don't want to play anymore."

Even Lasorda had cause for concern. For one of the few times in his outstanding managerial career, the fickle finger of failure was being pointed at him. If the Dodgers did any less than take the

National League West title, the implication was that Lasorda could well be looking for employment elsewhere. He was a seasoned veteran who had been around the game long enough to know the score. "They've got to blame somebody, and it might as well be the manager. That's the hazards of the job."

Fortunately, the Dodgers played better ball the second half. They would make up the five-game slack and battle the Rockies right down to the wire, before nailing down the West title the last week of September. The reacquisition of center-fielder Brett Butler from the Mets, and the inspired play of rookie infielder Chad Fonville, and a partially healthy Tim Wallach perked up the offense. Ramon Martinez and Ismael Valdes both had strong second halfs, while Todd Worrell proved an outstanding stopper.

As the season progressed, it became increasingly obvious that the heavy-hitting Colorado Rockies were for real. In just the third year of their franchise they looked like genuine contenders. The rivalry between the two clubs became one of the strongest in baseball. In a four-game series with the Rockies in Chavez Ravine, the Dodgers drew a total of 171,917 fans. "It's no secret the two teams don't like each other," Mike Piazza said after the two teams had traded first place six times in seven days.

Nomo's first post All-Star Game start on July 15 against the Florida Marlins was an encore performance. He was as sharp as ever. The previous night Dodger right-hander Ramon Martinez had thrown a no-hitter against the Marlins. The expansion Marlins had the second-worst record in the National League, and hoped to earn some respectability at the expense of Nomo. Some Dodger fans, delighted by the no-hitter, began checking to see the last time a team had thrown two consecutive no-hitters. (It was the St. Louis Browns in 1917.)

The ticket sales for Nomo's July 15 start against the Marlins numbered 45,449, nearly 15,000 more than for Martinez's no-hitter the night before. Nomo did not disappoint. The Marlins touched him for a hit in the second inning, removing all ideas of another no-hitter. But that was about all the offense they could muster. It was another masterful performance. With the exception of some minor trouble in the first inning, Nomo dominated the Marlins from start to finish. He opened the game by hitting leadoff man Quivio Veras. Veras stole second, and Chuck Carr sacrificed him to third. Veras scored when All-Star hero Jeff Conine lifted a sacrifice fly. No Marlin reached base again, until Veras singled with one out in the sixth. He stole second, and stayed there as Nomo struck out Chuck Carr and Jeff Conine to end the inning.

Nomo beat the Marlins 3–1 with a neat three-hitter for his seventh straight win. But what delighted him most was that he didn't issue a single walk. It was the first time since October 1, 1992, when he faced the Fukuoka Daiel Hawks in Japan, and the third time in his entire career that he hadn't walked a batter. His 10 strikeouts increased his league-leading total to 129. His record stood at 7–1, and he lowered his earned run average to 1.90. The Dodgers' record evened out at 36–36. It was the first time since June 25–26 that the Dodgers had won consecutive games.

Nomo also infused some energy into the crowd when he singled up the middle in the seventh inning for his first hit. It drew a standing ovation from the fans. Tommy Lasorda immediately jumped off the bench to taunt third baseman Tim Wallach. It seems that Lasorda had bet Wallach a sushi dinner for two that Nomo would get his first hit that game. When Wallach and Nomo crossed paths at the end of the inning, the Dodger third baseman uttered one word to Nomo, "Sushi." A delighted Nomo received the historic baseball in the clubhouse after the game. And you can be sure

Lasorda enjoyed winning his wager immensely. "Don't think I won't collect either," he said. "I'm going to eat at Moby Dick. It will cost Wallach a fortune."

The only downside was a hoax that had Dodger public relations director Jay Lucas livid. Radio station WQAM, the flagship station of the Florida Marlins, played an interview with someone pretending to be Hideo Nomo. The imposter ridiculed Marlins fans, saying that they didn't know the difference between sushi and a forkball. The problem was that no one on the station announced that it was a hoax, and the Marlins' office was flooded with calls.

Program director Andrew Ashwood said that no announcement was needed because he had introduced the imposter as "Nomo," not Hideo Nomo. He promised to reveal the hoax on his next show.

Five days later, the Dodgers invaded Joe Robbie Stadium. The hype was enormous. Large color advertisements in the local newspapers had Nomo pitted against All-Star MVP Jeff Conine. Nomo banter dominated the talk shows. There was even a hot-line number to learn how to cheer or request autographs in Japanese.

A crowd of 34,724 watched Nomo and the Marlins' Bobby Witt engage in a fine pitching duel. Witt was sharp, allowing five hits and striking out 12 in the seven innings he pitched, but the Dodgers defeated the Marlins 4–2 in 10 innings. Although Nomo didn't get the win, it was an important game for him. Without his best stuff he pitched eight strong innings, limiting the Marlins to four hits and striking out nine. "He showed how good a pitcher he was tonight," said Todd Worrell, who pitched a scoreless 10th inning for his 14th save. "He didn't have his good stuff, but while a lot of starters would be gone by the fifth, he kept us in the ball game for the whole way. That's what's so impressive about the guy."

It was the first time in his major league career that Nomo surrendered a lead, yielding a leadoff homer to shortstop Kurt Abbott in the fifth inning. But he bore down and kept his composure. The Marlins would touch him for only one more hit the rest of the night. Abbott's homer, his 10th of the year, ended Nomo's streak of 54 innings without issuing a home run.

Nomo received nothing but praise and respect from his teammates. "We don't expect him to be Superman," said Mike Piazza, "but he definitely set a standard for himself and he's living up to it.

168

He just gives you that confidence you're going to win every time he takes the mound."

Nomo watched the game from the clubhouse as first baseman Eric Karros won it for the Dodgers with a one-out single in the 10th to score Jose Offerman from second base. Roberto Kelly provided a two-run cushion with a bases-loaded sacrifice fly. When his teammates entered the clubhouse after the game, there was Nomo standing in the doorway shaking everyone's hand. This impressed pitching coach Dave Wallace to no end. "Can you believe that guy?" he said. "Just when you don't think you can't be more impressed by Nomo, he goes out and does something like this." The win halted a four-game Marlin winning streak, and improved the Dodgers' record to 38–39.

But bubbles burst in the heat of summer. And on the night of July 25, the Houston Astros became the first team in two months to defeat Nomo. Before a season-high crowd of 39,295 at the Astrodome, Doug Drabek threw a three-hit shutout to beat Nomo and the Dodgers 3–0, dropping the Dodgers to five games behind the Rockies. It was far from vintage Nomo. In four innings he allowed four hits and three earned runs. Most surprising, he struck out only one batter.

Nobody has ever accused Hideo Nomo of making excuses. But he later admitted to a crack on the fingernail of his middle finger, which prevented him from gripping his forkball properly.

"When I was pitching, it hurt," said Nomo. "You can understand just by watching today's game and how it affected me." Nomo, who had yielded only four runs in his last five starts combined, summoned Tommy Lasorda in the dugout and pointed at his finger. Lasorda hadn't known anything about it, and simply thought that Nomo was missing his good stuff. After seeing the nail, Lasorda felt it better not to take any chances. He removed Nomo from the game.

There were no alibis. In fact, he went out of his way to praise the Astros and assured everyone that he'd be ready for his next start against the Cincinnati Reds. According to trainer Bill Buhler, the plan was to treat the finger with the use of fingernail polish, and if necessary to apply a fake fingernail. Yet the game was a bitter pill. It ended Nomo's seven-game winning streak. He yielded more runs to the first three Houston hitters that night than he had in any of his previous six starts. Responding to Lasorda's decision to remove him from the game, Nomo was in full accord. "I couldn't have pitched anymore," he said simply.

His next outing was against the Reds on July 30. It was camera day at Dodger Stadium, and thousands of fans brought film and flashbulbs to the ballpark. The TV camera crews aired the game in Japan, where it was telecast live at 5:00 A.M. in downtown Tokyo, Osaka, Nagoya, Sapparo, Fukuoka, and Hiroshima.

There appeared to be no problem with the fingernail, and Nomo managed to build a 5–1 lead after eight innings, allowing the Reds but five hits while striking out eleven. The big controversy was Lasorda's decision to replace Nomo in the ninth inning, even with a healthy lead. Perhaps Lasorda was worried by the 99-degree heat and Nomo's 97 pitches. When he removed Nomo, who had yet to issue a walk, for pinch-hitter Mitch Webster, Lasorda was roundly booed by the sellout crowd of 53,085.

Even reliever Todd Worrell second-guessed Lasorda's decision. Worrell in relief gave up a three-run homer to first baseman Hal Morris in the ninth, before finally setting down the Reds. "I don't think I should have been in the game, but I don't make those decisions," Worrell said afterward. "I just don't think that was my spot to finish the game." The Dodgers' 5–4 win moved them within three games of the front-running Rockies.

Nomo's performance against the Reds was significant. That sore fingernail against Houston had limited Nomo to just one strikeout in four innings. It was a different story against the Reds. He struck out three of the first seven hitters he faced, including the dangerous Ron Gant, who looked foolish going after a forkball in the dirt. Nomo improved his record to 8–2, and became the first Dodger since Fernando Valenzuela to strike out ten or more batters in seven games. "It was just normal conditions," Nomo said through an interpreter when asked about his nail. "It didn't concern me. I would have been concerned if it started to crack."

Nomo brought a friend along to enjoy the game. He was Shuzo Matsuoka, the tennis star who had recently reached the Wimbledon quarterfinals and was entered in a tennis tournament at UCLA. This brought a little humor from *L.A. Times* columnist Mike Downey. "Had he won Wimbledon we could have had 'Shuzomania,' " Downey wrote. He also reported in the *Los Angeles Times* the recording of a new song called "The Ballad of Hideo Nomo," recorded by Hiroki and Saachiko, and available at music shops in Little Tokyo. "When you hear it, you might recognize the tune. The song's refrain is similar to Harry Belafonte's familiar 'Day-O, Day-Ay-O,' using Nomo's first name."

The true song would come in the month of August. It would be a mix of the high and the low. To borrow a bit from Charles Dickens, "it was the best of times and the worst of times." August found Hideo Nomo at the very best of his game and also at his very worst.

# 11

# The Dog Days of August

The best of times was the weekend of August 5–6. Two major league pitchers, each Japanese, separated by a generation, came together under the same roof. The lingering memories of the occasion are etched indelibly in the thoughts of all involved.

The night of August 5, 1995, Hideo Nomo nearly touched immortality as he barely missed a no-hit game, shutting out the Giants 3–0 in Candlestick Park before a crowd of 43,167. The same evening a handsome and fit 51-year-old Masanori Murakami was honored at home plate by the San Francisco Giants for whom 30 years earlier he had toiled as a pitcher.

It was a special moment for Karen Kinoshita, a

third-generation Japanese American and director of catering at the Miyako Hotel in San Francisco's Japantown, where the Murakami reception was held the following day. She is a lifelong baseball fan, her father taking her to her first ball game at Candlestick Park in 1965, ironically on a day when 20-year-old Masanori Murakami was pitching for the Giants.

"It was very exciting," she recalls. "I had never been to a professional game, and since then I have always been a Giant fan. I never really drew the connection to Masanori Murakami. I was just excited about the game. It wasn't until later years that I realized how lucky I was to see the first Japanese player. I don't think I understood the importance of that until recently when Nomo came. We didn't have these kind of heroes when I was a kid."

The *Los Angeles Times* sports pages featured concurrent photos of the left-hander Murakami and right-hander Nomo, each tossing a pitch. Nomo was returning to Candlestick Park, the site of his debut three months earlier. Murakami was here at the invitation of the Giants, spending a week with the Japanese community, who 30 years ago welcomed him as a hero.

Nomo pitched a masterpiece. He struck out 11

San Francisco batters, and all that prevented him from hurling a no-hitter was a two-out infield single in the seventh inning by Giant shortstop Royce Clayton. By the fifth inning Nomo had won the hearts of the most loyal of Giant faithfuls, especially an extremely proud Asian community. "The Japanese Americans here in the Bay area have mixed feelings. We root for the Giants, but we want to see Nomo do well," says Babe Utzumi. "All the Asian people are cheering him on, especially here in the West Coast."

Nomo breezed through the first 6⅔ innings with ease until he walked Giant first baseman Mark Carreon on a full count. Shortstop Royce Clayton was next. He had been hitless in seven at-bats against Nomo, fanning five times. Nomo had a count of 1 and 2 on Clayton. Nomo's next pitch was a ball, evening the count to 2 and 2. This prompted Giant manager Dusty Baker to make a critical decision. He decided to send Carreon running on the next pitch.

As Carreon took off, Clayton slapped the ball into the gap between short and third. Dodger shortstop Jose Offerman, realizing that he had no play at second, planted his feet firmly and fired to first. Royce Clayton beat the throw by a half step, drawing a mixed reaction of cheers and groans.

Again, Nomo was his stoic self. He took a deep breath, struck out Kurt Manwaring on four pitches, and never gave up another hit. To ice the day's joy, Nomo drove in his first run with a two-out single in the ninth off Shawn Barton.

The partisan Giant crowd rallied to Nomo, giving him a rousing ovation when he took the mound in the bottom of the ninth, chanting his name through the final three outs. It was more than an Asian affair too. Giant fans were simply paying homage and respect to a pitcher who had shut them out for 23 innings during the season, allowing just four hits and striking out 31 batters.

The Giants fans had broken into the traditional "Beat L.A." chant early in the game when the Dodgers took a quick 2–0 lead. But they changed their tune by the fifth when it looked like a Nomo no-hitter was possible. When Nomo struck out Robbie Thompson to end the sixth, a huge ovation ensued as umpire Joe West raised his right arm for a called third strike. By the seventh they were cheering each strike, holding tight.

Glenallen Hill's pop-up nearly dropped between second baseman Chad Fonville and right fielder Raul Mondesi, until Mondesi stuck out his glove at the last moment to catch the ball. If any more need be said, let's just say that Nomo's two base hits that night were more than he allowed the entire Giant team.

For Giant shortstop Royce Clayton, his seventh-inning single taught him something. "At first I only went 1 for 7 against him. Since then I've gone 3 for 3," Clayton said later in the year. "Now I tend to be more still, and look for good pitches to hit. A lot of times that fork splits and it can drop any way. Rarely do I see him strike out a guy on a good pitch." But Clayton still felt that Nomo had shown him better stuff in the past. "I've seen him have better command as far as his splitter . . . [but] he had a lot giddy-up on his fastball and seemed to throw it well. He had enough control and velocity on his fastball to get guys out, and that's what he did."

Matt Williams, who was still sitting out his injury, said basically the same thing, but a bit more succinctly. "Nomo knows how to pitch. Pitching is just the art of deception. I'm sure he'll learn even more."

But it was Fred Claire, the Dodgers executive vice president, who probably revealed the most. Admitting that the Dodgers had taken some flack in February with their $2 million gamble, Claire told the *Los Angeles Times* that Nomo had a "presence" about him, the presence of a winner, and that Nomo had put everything on the table—fame, fortune, and all of life's conveniences—to risk playing against the best. Nomo said to Claire at the time, "I haven't proven anything. I've done nothing." "That impressed me. That impressed me a lot!" Claire said.

He also revealed something entirely new. It had to do with the two-minute video that the Dodgers looked at before signing Nomo to such a large bonus. It said a lot.

"You guys would have had me six feet under ground. The stories [about] giving him $2 million without seeing him. . . . I didn't want to say it at the time, but one of the scenes on the film clip was at the All-Star game with the manager taking him out of the game. Well, he had a kind of a good look on his face."

Nomo was his usual matter-of-fact self when talking about the game. "I could have kept going like that for several more innings," he said. "I knew I hadn't allowed a hit, but I wasn't thinking about a no-hitter." By tossing his third shutout of the year, Nomo increased his record to 9–2, while lowering his ERA to 1.89, the second best in the National League. He also increased his league-leading strikeout total to 161.

The celebration and reception for Masanori Murakami was something very special as well. It was called "Giant Day" in Japantown, and there was a big commotion for Murakami. The only concern was that August 6 was the anniversary of the dropping of the atomic bomb on Hiroshima. What is interesting is that while they wanted Makamuri's day to really be his, they also wanted Nomo there too, because the community had waited thirty years for a hero like him. "We took such pride that Nomo had made an immediate impact on all cultures. We really took pride in him. On the other hand, we didn't want to overshadow the fact that the person who started this off was Murakami," says Karen Kinoshita.

The months of August and September would see the Los Angeles Dodgers and Colorado Rockies battle to the wire for the National League West title. In its Major League Report Power Rankings (August 2–8), *USA Today: Baseball Weekly* ranked the Dodgers tenth among the 28 teams with 110 points. The Colorado Rockies were ranked seventh (132 points). Yet the San Diego Padres' Tony Gwynn broke traditional ranks by insisting that the Dodgers were the team to beat in the NL West. The Padres had routed the Dodgers earlier in the year, and the Dodgers were still struggling. Nevertheless, the National League batting champ sent out a warning.

"It's disgusting how good they are. My God, Raul Mondesi is batting sixth. And the scary part for the rest of us is that they're going to be around for a long time. They've got that intimidating lineup, that great pitching—it reminds me of those Dodger teams in the glory years. If someone's going to beat those guys, they better do it this year, before those guys become unbeatable."

In *Baseball Weekly*'s Power Report section, Nomo trailed Greg Maddux 30 points to 13 in the Cy Young ratings, with the Reds' John Smiley third with 7 points. For National League Rookie of the Year Nomo captured 28 points (including 5 of the 6 first-place votes), to 13 for the Braves' Chipper Jones. A photo of Nomo appeared directly below that of the Reds' Ron Gant—then considered the leading candidate for league MVP—with the following caption: "After a good manicure, he was back to All-Star form."

A cursory look shows how touch-and-go the National League West race became during the dog days of August. Entering the month of August, the Dodgers were 45–42, three games behind the Colorado Rockies. On August 5, following Nomo's magnificent game against the Giants, they were three and a half behind with a 48–44 record. On August 12, the two teams were dead even at 52–46. Three days later on August 15, after winning 7 of their last 10 games, the Dodgers moved one game ahead of the Rockies with a record of 54–47.

From June 2 to August 5 Nomo reeled off an amazing exhibition of pitching, even more impressive considering his first five starts resulted in five no-decisions. His 9–2 mark included seven straight wins. In 95⅓ innings he struck out 112 batters. His ERA was a microscopic 1.23. He went the distance four times and had double-digit strikeouts seven different times.

When he took the mound against the Cardinals on August 10, he still looked sharp. Except for solo homers by Brian Jordan leading off the second, and a two-out shot by Mark Sweeney in the fourth, Nomo allowed only four more hits in the eight innings he pitched, walking three and striking out seven. But if Nomo looked good, the same cannot be said for the Dodger fans. The game wasn't even played to a conclusion. Umpire Jim Quick called a forfeit with one out in the bottom of the ninth, because fans threw baseballs onto the field after being told to desist from doing so two times before.

In plain baseball lingo, it was three strikes and you're out.

While the Dodger management expressed regret over the barrage of pitching practice from the stands, they still questioned the fairness of the forfeit. But there were more than baseballs being peppered actually. Said Cardinals right-fielder John Mabry: "I wasn't too worried until a bottle of Southern Comfort flew out of the stands and hit me. I got hit by a rum bottle too." The Dodgers filed an official protest with the National League office. But Cardinal pitching coach Bob Gibson, who was known to throw a few close ones from the pitching mound himself during his brilliant career, was not sympathetic. The fans in Dodger Stadium had clearly crossed the line of appropriate behavior. "The Dodger fans used to be among the best in baseball," Gibson said. "I'm afraid you can't say that anymore."

With the forfeit, Nomo's record fell to 9–3, and the Dodgers fell one game behind the Rockies. But more than anything it said something about a game that seemed to be getting more in tune to the violence of the times: the Angels' Chili Davis going into the stands after an angry fan who insulted him; an irate Chicago Cub fan charging on the field to take on Randy Myers for throwing a home run pitch; and Dodger baseball fans making a mockery of "free baseball day" by peppering the opposing players.

National League vice-president Katy Feeney responded to the Dodger protest with a statement reading in part, "Obviously it was not the way you want to end the ballgame, but the umpires decided in their judgment that the situation was out of control. They weren't protecting just the players, but the fans too."

Cardinal manager Mike Jorgenson felt the umpires made the right decision. He was legitimately concerned about his team's safety. "I think most of my players, when they realized what was happening, were relieved by the decision," he said. Sitting in the third row of the boxes with playwright Neil Simon was agent Dennis Gilbert. "It got pretty nasty," commented Gilbert. "We looked up, and there were balls flying right over our heads. It was outrageous. It was a disgrace to baseball." Perhaps the Dodgers' Chris Gwynn summed up the lunacy best after he was hit in the head with an apple while he was standing in the on-deck circle. "It was the weirdest thing I've ever seen," said Gwynn. "I've been hit by worse things in San Francisco, but these are your own fans."

Nonetheless, the Dodgers showed some spunk on the ball field. The following night, Ismael Valdes, with ninth-inning help from Todd Worrell, who recorded his 23rd save, pitched the Dodgers to a 3–2 win over the Pirates, and a first-place tie with the Rockies. The Dodgers kept on pace the following night, pounding out 17 hits, including a pair of Mike Piazza homers and four Eric Karros RBIs, beating the Pirates 11–10 in eleven innings.

On August 13, 1995, a slice of baseball history vanished as Micky Mantle died from cancer at the age of 60. He once hit a home run at Griffith Stadium, Washington, in 1953 that measured at 565 feet. Some experts say there has never been one hit any farther. That same day in the "Dodgers on Deck" section of the *L.A. Times*, the schedule was set for the three-game series against the Chicago Cubs to begin on August 14.

By winning five of the first six games in their current nine-game home stand, the Dodgers moved into first place with a record of 54–46. Tom Candiotti was due to start against the Cubs' Frank Castillo on Monday, with Nomo slated to go against Steve Trachsel on Tuesday. Things looked promising. Yet at the top of the Dodger update there was glitch. It read, "Although pitcher Hideo Nomo experienced some stiffness in his right elbow after his last start, he is still scheduled to start Tuesday night."

When a pattern of excellence seems to fade, no matter what the arena, seers and sages look for reasons. Clearly if the 1995 baseball season had ended on August 10 instead of early October, the saga of Hideo Nomo would have ended without a blemish. The fact that it didn't only adds to the drama of the story. Because happy endings never really end with perfection. Hard times and travail are needed to build upon. And Hideo Nomo was only human.

Whether it be overwork, too many pitches, the alleged elbow stiffness, a plethora of media hype, or late-season jitters, the ten days from August 15 to August 25 were Nomo's worst of the year. Not only did he get beat in two of his three starts, he was suddenly hittable. The number of earned runs he allowed per nine innings increased appreciably, and the comment around the league was that Nomo might be losing his magic. In these three mid-August starts, Nomo gave up 17 runs, hitting rock bottom on August 25 in Philadelphia when the Phillies rocked him for seven runs on six hits in just three innings—his shortest stint of the season.

On August 15, Nomo picked up his tenth win as the Dodgers beat the Cubs 7–5. The crowd of

48,449 saw the Dodgers extend their division lead to a season-high two games over the Rockies. More than 2,000 fans flew from Japan to see Hideo Nomo live. But even by his own admission, Nomo wasn't up to snuff. He gave the Cubs three runs in the first inning, and by the sixth he had already given up a season-high 10 hits. It was the second highest total of runs Nomo had allowed in a game all season, and the most since May 11, 1994, against the Seibu Lions while still pitching in Japan.

He was fortunate to get help from the dazzling play of right fielder Raul Mondesi. He blasted his first career grand slam homer in the fourth inning, hit a sacrifice fly to the fence in the sixth inning, singled and stole second in the eighth inning, and threw out Brian McRae at second base with a perfect peg in the fifth.

Nomo insisted that while he had been bothered by a sore elbow, the injury gave him little trouble that day. But there were troubling indicators. He threw 118 pitches in the 6⅔ innings he pitched, yielding five runs (four earned) and 11 hits. He was lucky to get the win, as Todd Worrell pitched a 1-2-3 ninth inning to record his 25th save.

Yet there was still room for levity. Remembering back to July 15, when Tommy Lasorda bet Tim Wallach that Nomo would get his first big-league hit against the Marlins, it was payback time. True to his word, Wallach shelled out $140 for a sushi lunch to pay off his bet to Lasorda and Nomo. Never at a loss for a few words or a good meal, a fine time was had by all. "Hideo and I ate a lot of raw fish," Lasorda said. "We really put the big hurt on him. Hideo and I cleaned him out."

Of course, it was a Japanese restaurant, and Nomo brought the patrons to a standstill by his very presence. "You stop to think about what this guy's been through," Lasorda said, "and it's just incredible. Here's a guy who technically defected from their baseball program, and now he's a hero over there. The most significant part is that for thirty years the Japanese didn't know how their players compared to ours. What he's done has been a big boost to their baseball program."

The following day, August 18, the Dodgers bolstered their pennant hopes by trading for Brett Butler, reacquiring him from the Mets for two highly regarded minor leaguers. Since letting him go five months earlier, the Dodgers had tried five different leadoff men in an attempt to replace Butler. The Dodgers were so euphoric with his return to the lineup that they walked up to Fred Claire and began shaking his hand and slapping his back. "We should win this now, no?" said a happy Raul Mondesi. "We've got everything. We've got speed. We've got offense. We've got defense. We're the team to beat."

But the Dodgers also had problems, problems about to embarrass them no end. They were heading to Shea Stadium for a three-game series against the last-place Mets. By the time they left, the Mets had swept them all three games.

"I guess we put a crimp in Nomomania, didn't we," said an elated Dallas Green after his team defeated Nomo and the Dodgers 5–3 on August 20. Green's euphoria is easily understood considering that it had been three years since the Mets had swept the Dodgers at Shea Stadium. Clearly the Mets had played some good baseball, as indicated by their 20–16 record since the All-Star break, and by embarrassing Nomo and the Dodgers they captured their 10th victory in their last 13 games.

But as Ira Berkow in his *New York Times* column noted: "In Any Language, This Wasn't Finest Hour for Nomomania." Nomo himself broadly concurred, describing the outing as "the worst." The loss to the Mets again dropped the Dodgers into a first-place tie with the Rockies, and was an understandable disappointment for the 10,000 Japanese and Japanese American fans who had come to Shea Stadium to cheer Nomo on. It was something that played upon Nomo's mind as well. Attired in a cool tan suit and a yellow and blue tie, he was asked if he was aware of the large number of Japanese fans in a Shea Stadium crowd that numbered 33,668.

"There's a lot of expectation about me, I feel," he said. "I know they expect me to be a pretty good pitcher." Many fans that day embarked from the subway at Shea with Japanese newspapers folded under their arms. Others carried banners with Japanese lettering. At game time, the public address announcers prepared to give the lineups in both English and Japanese. There was the usual "K" corner at the upper deck of Shea Stadium to cheer Nomo, just as there had been when young Dwight Gooden was mowing down batters ten years earlier. The difference was that Gooden was a hometown strikeout king, and Nomo was striking out hometown heroes, 13 to be exact.

And here was the big puzzle. Nomo called it his worst outing, yet he fanned 13 batters and gave up only two walks on six hits in seven innings. If his strikeout pitch was working, something else must be missing. Nomo insisted that his elbow wasn't the problem, that he felt no pain. But his fastball did lack its usual zip. Rarely did the speed gun register at 90 mph or more. He allowed only six hits, but according to opposing hitters they were all fastballs. Moreover, three of the six hits he surrendered were homers, and home runs had previously been rare off Nomo.

Nomo, who had gone six successive starts at one point without yielding a home run, gave up two homers in four pitches against the Mets. There was a three-run shot by Jose Vizcaino in the third, then two pitches later Carl Everett made it back-to-back homers in a four-run third inning. During his prior starts Nomo had given up two homers in a game twice, and his only three-homer game had been at Coors Field, Denver, where the air blows thin.

"If you noticed, all of our hits came on fastballs," noted Everett. "That's not a coincidence." "[Nomo's] tough," Everett went on to say. "You don't want to get to that split-finger. That . . . is nasty. You have to sit on the fastball and wait for it. Otherwise, he's unhittable. You're just not going to hit that split-finger. He'll kill you."

Had the Dodgers been relying too much on Nomo? Had his earlier success magnified a myth of the invincible? Some of Nomo's teammates seemed to think so. "There are going to be times he runs into a little trouble," said Eric Karros, who went hitless in 12 at-bats in the series. "You can't expect him to flirt with a no-hitter every time. . . . I mean, he's human."

Chad Fonville, starting his first game in left field, saw the Met sweep as a team failing. "Just because Nomo's pitching, you can't sit back. Everyone's going to have games like that once in a while. . . . We didn't play good ball. You don't score runs, you don't win. It doesn't matter who's pitching."

But the numbers for the week said something. Nomo made two starts, winning one and losing one. He pitched 13⅔ innings and struck out 20, yet his earned run average for the week was a whopping 5.93. His record now stood at 10 wins and 4 losses. He led the National League with 188 strikeouts, but his earned run average was shooting up. It was still a respectable 2.28, but the ERA gap between him and Greg Maddux had widened.

"There's not any pitcher that's perfect," said Fred Claire. "I think he threw the ball well. There's no evidence of any [elbow] problem at all. When a guy strikes out 13, that's evidence there's no problem. If the expectation is perfection, that's more than can be obtained."

It might be argued Nomo's outing against the Mets was more a bad inning—a four-run second—

than a disastrous start. Claire's suggestion there-
fore was well taken. Nomo's fastball might have
lost some velocity, but the only other run resulted
from Butch Huskey's solo home run in the seventh.

He might not have been sharp, but six hits and
two walks in seven innings is not exactly the end
of the world. But there could be no excuse for the
disaster of August 25, when Nomo went against
the Philadelphia Phillies. "Perfection" suddenly
became a moot issue. Nomo was simply terrible.

Nothing worked as the Phillies battered Nomo
for seven runs (five earned) and six hits in just
three innings, thumping the Dodgers by a score of
17–4. All eyes instead were on Phillies first baseman Gregg Jefferies, who hit for the cycle (single,
double, triple, homer), to become the first Philadelphia Phillie to do so in 32 years.

"Nomo Magic Might Be Disappearing," Rick
Lawes wrote in the August 30 issue of *USA Today
Baseball Weekly*. The number of earned runs per
nine innings had gone up measurably in his last
four starts, including a horrendous 15.00 ERA in
his August 25 start against the Phillies. In his last
four outings he had gone 1–3, allowing 17 runs in
his last three starts. Before Nomo's last start in
Philadelphia, Phillies manager Jim Fregosi said

that in scouting Nomo, his observers noted he was showing signs of a sore arm, with all the stress his delivery puts on his arm.

"I just think he's a little tired," said catcher Mike Piazza. "He's thrown a lot of pitches for us. The fastball is a little off, and he's struggling with his location." He was barely hitting 90 mph by the radar gun, and had already thrown 153 innings of big league baseball. He had pitched only 114 innings in Japan the year before, when tendonitis in his right shoulder forced him to miss the last half of the 1994 season.

The Dodgers had another concern. The media hype, ever present, had become somewhat of a circus. While his attraction in Japan was well documented, the Dodgers feared that the band of 50 or so journalists who traveled with the Dodgers to report on Nomo's every move was taking its toll. In the United States the tradition is that the starting pitcher does not talk to the press at all prior to the game. Yet Nomo was still talking to the Japanese press up to forty minutes before game time. "We're going to try to minimize all of this and try to keep everyone away from him," said Lasorda. But it would be a tall order, easier said than done.

"I just think [Nomo] is doing too much," right-fielder Raul Mondesi said. "A half hour before the game, he's got ten people around his locker. People have got to leave him alone." Many of his teammates were becoming miffed themselves. When the team came out for pre-batting practice stretching, there was evident disgust when they saw the huge black cameras awaiting Nomo's appearance at the end of the dugout.

The press here found Nomo his usual shy self, hiding behind the responses interpreted by Michael Nomura, who traveled every day with the Dodgers. "Sometimes, when I threw bad pitches, we would win," Nomo said. "I have to learn mistakes from the way I pitched, and just try to help the team."

Yet through it all the Dodgers were still in a pennant fight, sparring back and forth with the stubborn Colorado Rockies. By August 30, the Atlanta Braves had all but wrapped up the National League East, with a fourteen-game lead over the second-place Phillies. The Cincinnati Reds had an enormous 13½ game lead over the Houston Astros in the National League Central. But the National League West was up for grabs.

The Dodgers and Rockies were again tied for the division lead with identical records of 60–56. Once more it was Nomo to the rescue. On August 31 he helped to celebrate his 27th birthday against the

Mets by showing the crowd of 47,997 at Dodger Stadium that his arm was sound. He pitched 7⅓ innings of shutout baseball, allowing two hits, walking two and striking out 11. When he left the game with a cracked fingernail, it was with a 5–0 lead. However, his teammates could not hold the lead, and the Mets tied the game with five of their own in the top of the ninth.

The Dodgers won it in the bottom of the inning when Brett Butler crossed the plate with the winning run. He had led off with a single down the left-field line, stole second, and went to third on Jose Offerman's single to left. After Mike Piazza was intentionally walked, Eric Karros lifted a soft liner to shallow center field. When Met center-fielder Ryan Thompson dropped the ball after the catch, Butler raced home to secure a 6–5 Dodger win.

But there was more to the story. Butler had led the array of outspoken Dodgers when management decided to bring up Mike Busch, when Tim Wallach went down with a knee injury earlier in the month. The appearance of Busch, a replacement player during the strike, caused a ruckus among Dodger players for whom Busch was nothing less than a scab of the worst kind.

Led by Butler, the players were furious, voting

unanimously in their rejection of Busch. But it seems Dodger fans thought otherwise. They were disgusted by the behavior of their millionaire players acting like "baby brats," and Busch drew a chord of thunderous cheers at Dodger Stadium, while Butler was roundly booed. But peace prevailed that night when Butler made up with Busch, told him his feelings were nothing personal, and scored the game-winning run. The degree of sincerity might have been murky, but the Dodgers managed to pull a half game ahead of the Rockies.

The Labor Day holiday would soon mark the traditional passing of summer. Football was in the air, and in the Bay area of northern California most eyes were on the Raiders and the Forty-Niners. However, for the first time since the 1940s, when the Cleveland Rams moved its franchise west to Los Angeles, the city was without a professional football team. The Rams had relocated to St. Louis, while the enigmatic Al Davis had returned his Raiders to their beloved Oakland. Baseball still ruled supreme in Los Angeles, while the O. J. Simpson trial kept the City of Angels in the camera eye throughout the nation and the world.

With a wild-card berth looming as well should the title escape the Dodgers, there was still plenty of baseball to watch. It would take the entire month of September before the cards would play themselves out. When the final hand was dealt, it was the right arm of Hideo Nomo, the "Tornado" from Japan, who put the Dodgers in the National League playoffs for the first time since 1988.

# 12

# Autumn and September

**N**omo and the Dodgers had both survived those dog days of August. On September 1, the Dodgers' record stood at 61–56, and they held a slim half-game lead over the Rockies. But there was one glaring difference. The Dodgers were 30–27 at home and 31–29 on the road. The Rockies, on the other hand, were a far stronger team at home. At Coors Stadium they sported a 35–24 record. On the road they were 25–32. Moreover, the schedule had the Rockies finishing the season at home against the Giants, while the Dodgers would finish out on the road in San Diego.

As we have seen, Nomo was his best and his worst during the month of August. When he was hot as a pistol in June, the Dodgers were loudly predicting that they might run away with the National League West. Confidence increased in late July when they acquired pitchers Kevin Tampani and Mark Guthrie. With the addition of Brett Butler on August 18, the Dodgers finally acquired the leadoff man they had been searching for since they let Butler go early in the year.

All year long the Dodgers had been baseball's most notorious underachievers. The pressing question seemed to be how badly they wanted to win. The talent was there, especially with Butler filling that much needed void. Yet something (or things) was not working well. Dodger announcer Vin Sculley had been around the game for a long time, and he too was perplexed. "Sometimes you look at what should be a teriffic ball club and it just doesn't come together," he said.

Too many games had been slipping away. This has never been a good sign. The Dodgers traditionally have had a celebrity aura to cope with. After all, Los Angeles was show biz and tinsel town, and the Dodgers were definitely Los Angeles. There had always been a useless array of hangers-on around the clubhouse, "greenflies," the players called them. All this predated the Nomomania of 1995. The press in other cities seemed to delight in taking its share of pot shots at Lasorda and his players.

Now the skipper himself seemed to be in trouble. Whispers had it that relations between Lasorda and Fred Claire were far from the best. Lasorda was still unsigned for 1996, an indication that 1995 might be his last.

Nomo may have struggled some, losing three out of four in late August, but he seemingly regained his composure. On September 1, he far outdistanced the pack in strikeouts, and his ERA was second only to Maddux. With Colorado hanging so close all year long, it is a good bet to say that had it not been for "The Tornado," 1995 would have been the "Year of the Rockies" in the National League West.

When Nomo started against the Phillies on September 5, his biggest concern was a sore fingernail that had limited him to seven shutout innings against the Mets his last time out. His record stood at 10–5. He had pitched 160.1 innings, and allowed only 99 hits and 44 earned runs. Ramon Martinez (14–7) and Ismael Valdes (11–9) had registered more wins, but had not been involved in nearly as many no-decisions. Nomo's 2.47 ERA was by far the best among Dodger starters, the only starter with an ERA under 3.00. His 205 K's were tops in the National League.

Critics may have commented on his control, but the facts indicate otherwise. Sure, he threw a lot of pitches, but he clearly outdistanced the other Dodger starters when it came to strikeout/walk ratio. His 205 K's vs. 65 walks put him 140 on the surplus side in strikeouts. By comparison Valdes was 78 on the surplus side and Martinez was 47. The fourth starter, Tom Candiotti, had struck out 76 more batters than he walked.

*USA Today Baseball Weekly*'s Power Rankings for the week of September 6–12 ranked Nomo second to Greg Maddux in Cy Young voting, 30 points to 18 (on a 5–3–1 basis—with Maddux getting all six first-place votes). Pete Schourek of the Cincinnati Reds placed a distant third with only three points. National League Rookie of the Year was a dead tie between Nomo and the Braves' Chipper Jones. Nomo and Jones had 24 points apiece, splitting the first-place votes with three each. Ismael Valdes was a far distant third with three points.

"Deadlock," was what *Baseball Weekly* called it. "Our staff couldn't decide on who should be NL Rookie of the Year at this point. Chipper Jones . . . has been a clutch No. 3 hitter, and steady third baseman for Atlanta. Hideo Nomo has lived up to the hype, anchoring the Los Angeles Dodger rotation in the pennant race."

On September 5, 1995, Cal Ripken, Jr., tied Lou Gehrig's longstanding record by playing in his 2,130th consecutive game for the Baltimore Orioles. Ripken, one of the game's true leaders and outstanding role models, would break Gehrig's record the following night.

That same September 5, Atlanta's Greg Maddux became the majors' first 16-game winner, lifting his record to an incredible 16–2. Bob Verducci of *Sports Illustrated* would argue at the end of the year that Maddux was the greatest right-hander in 75 years, since the glory days of Walter Johnson. That might be stretching the point too far, but little doubt remained that he had become baseball's best hurler since the heyday of Koufax, Marichal, Gibson, Seaver, and Carlton. Maddux not only assured himself a fourth straight Cy Young Award, but a great shot at National League MVP honors as well.

Nomo did well against the Phillies on September 5, his 24th start of the season. But again his fingernail sidelined him, this time after just five innings. "I broke it in the same place," said Nomo. "When I break a nail, I can't pitch as well as I'd like to." Yet he allowed the Phillies only one run on three hits, and be broke something else that night. His seven strikeouts give him 212 on the year, a new Dodger rookie record.

Brett Butler provided the impetus for the Dodgers' 2–1 win, drawing a walk to drive in the game-winning run in the ninth inning. The Dodgers were now 64–58, and opened a one-game lead over the Rockies and a four-game lead over the surging San Diego Padres. But another potential win in the Nomo ledger ended instead in a one more no-decision contest.

Nomo's cheapest shot came one week later. It was not the result of an errant fastball or faulty control, a balk or a wild pitch too many, or even a forkball that didn't bend. It did not come from the bat of a Fred McGriff or a Tony Gwynn. Rather the "shot" was an intemperate comment with racial overtones by Chicago Cub announcer Harry Caray that had some people buzzing.

On September 12 against the Cubs, Nomo showed no ill effects of his cracked fingernail. He was solid and steady in pitching the Dodgers to a 7–1 win in his Wrigley Field debut. Lifting his record to 11–5, Nomo yielded six hits and one run in eight innings of work. He struck out eight, including three of the first four batters he faced. He walked no one.

"He's back," said Mike Piazza, grinning. "You could tell right away he had that extra pop on his fastball. Obviously we need him healthy. We're going to need him down the stretch." Piazza, it should be added, went 3 for 5 with three RBIs to lift his batting average to .363. With 16 games left in the season, he was in a position to become the first catcher since Ernie Lombardi in 1942 to lead either league in hitting.

By the second inning the Dodgers had staked Nomo to a 5–0 lead, with seven hits—including two each by Brett Butler, Chad Fonville, and Piazza. Butler's inspired play in center field had Nomo in complete awe. With a 6–0 lead and runners on second and third in the eighth, Nomo watched as Howard Johnson's long drive headed toward the center-field ivy. Butler kept running back, looking over his shoulder as he ran, caught the ball, and slammed face first into the brick wall. He collapsed to the ground, threw the ball into the infield, and went down again.

Nomo lost his shutout as Rey Sanchez scored from third after Butler's catch. When the inning ended, Nomo stood on the field waiting to high-five Butler, who at age 38 still shows a lot of younger fellows the way baseball is meant to be played.

The victory was the Dodgers' seventh in their last nine games, remaining one game behind the Rockies and two games ahead of the Houston Astros in the wild-card race. However, the Dodgers were looking title, not wild card. This Lasorda made clear. "If we're a wild-card team, we won't be doing any celebrating," said Delino DeShields. "We'll be happy we're in the playoffs, but that's nothing to celebrate." Or as Mike Piazza clearly indicated, "We're not supposed to pop champagne for being a wild-card team."

According to Nomo's agent, Don Nomura, nothing meant more to Nomo than the possibility of playing in a World Series. "You don't know how badly he wants this," said Nomura. "This is very very important to him. He wants to help the Dodgers get into the World Series."

The Harry Caray incident was unfortunate at best and downright stupid at worst. The controversy resulted from a broadcast comment during Caray's pre-game interview with Chicago Cub manager Jim Rigglemann. The two were talking about Nomo's sensational rookie year when Caray said, "Well, my eyes are slanty enough, how about yours?" To compound matters, Caray steadfastly refused to say he was sorry. "What's wrong with saying his eyes are slanty?" Caray said three days later. "How about when you talk about a fighter with a broken nose or cauliflower ears? You use it as a descriptive phrase, don't you?"

Understandably the Japanese American Citizens League found obvious fault. And they are not known as an organization that looks for racial slurs behind every locked door. "I don't think he says any of these things with real malicious intent," said William Yoshino, the league's director. "But the fact is that it goes out over the airways for public consumption, and it reinforces the use of racial slurs to people who don't know better."

Moreover, according to Yoshino this was not the first incident involving Caray. "About ten years ago, he used the word Jap on the air. It is considered a racial slur, and we wrote a letter complaining about it at the time."

Caray's bosses at WGN radio issued an apology, but he remained steadfast, insisting "I didn't do anything wrong." Said WGN general manager Dan Fabian: "Knowing Harry, the guy doesn't have a mean bone in his body, so I can't believe he would have said or done anything to intentionally hurt someone." Rick Telander of the *Chicago Sun Times* urged Caray to apologize, insisting an apology would make, "all OK," and stating that he believes that "Harry is no racist."

Caray's remarks didn't sit well with the Asian community on the West Coast either. Babe Utusumi in his "Random Thoughts" column in the *Hokubei Mainichi* let his feelings be known. He wrote:

> The temerity of Chicago's baseball broadcasting icon, Harry Caray, in describing Hideo Nomo as a slant-eyed pitcher a few weeks ago was truly a cheap shot. I'm surprised he didn't throw in "with buck teeth."
>
> The Nikkei population in the United States is so small that Caray must have figured he could get away with that kind of slander. Would he have the guts to describe a black center-fielder as thicked-lipped and frizzled-haired? Or a Jewish first baseman big-nosed? Or a bald-headed white American at third? To this day Caray has refused to apologize for his remark.

Hideo Nomo needed no revenge. As the 1995 season entered its final two weeks, he had enjoyed remarkable success. And while many observers might say his fastball was no longer popping as it had earlier in the year, it must be noted too that he was averaging 110 pitches each time out and already had pitched in excess of 50 more innings than the previous year, when shoulder trouble sidelined him most of the second half of the season.

Nomo steadfastly refused to say he was tired, although catcher Mike Piazza could see the loss of zip from his fastball. And while opposing hitters better learned to sniff out and wait on the fastball, Nomo's forkball remained as baffling as ever. Nomo, in fact, had no greater fan than Piazza, his All-Star battery mate. "Nomo has been outstanding for so long, he can't slip up once in a while without it being a federal case. Unless you're Greg Maddux, it's going to happen to everybody."

If Nomo played hurt, he rarely revealed pain. After the Mets game when he first cracked his fingernail, Piazza noticed that it was broken almost all the way down to the cuticle. Yet when a small group of English-speaking reporters gathered at Nomo's locker after the game and asked for a peek at the damaged finger, Nomo covered his right hand with his left and said through his interpreter, "No!" Another reporter asked for a quick look. Again Nomo's response through his interpreter was an unwavering "No!" He stood and walked out, carefully keeping his hand concealed. He would give away nothing.

When Nomo made his next start against the Giants on September 19, it was 25 years exactly since Gaylord Perry had hurled his fourth consecutive shutout for the San Francisco Giants. Of all the teams which Nomo had faced from May through August, the Giants had been his easiest target. He had thrown 23 innings, allowed no runs, and tossed complete-game shutouts his last two outings against them. This time, however, the Giants had Nomo's number. Nomo lasted only five innings as the Giants trounced the Dodgers 7–2.

The Giants went to work fast against Nomo, scoring a pair of runs in the top of the first. Then made it 3–0 with a run in the third. The Dodgers scored solo runs in the bottoms of the third and fourth to close the gap 3–2. From the start, Nomo was wanting. He walked both Deion Sanders and Barry Bonds in the opening moments. Matt Williams's run-scoring single and Mark Carreon's sacrifice fly accounted for the two runs. In the third a wild pitch resulted in yet another run.

By the fifth inning he looked like he had settled down. Barry Bonds looked bad as Nomo got him on a weak pop foul. Matt Williams was next. Nomo threw a wicked change-up past the slugging third baseman, fanning Williams for the second out.

Suddenly things changed. With two outs Mark Carreon singled to right. Glenallen Hill followed with a broken-bat single to put men on first and second. Shortstop Royce Clayton, who had hit Nomo well of late, walked to fill the bases. Up came catcher Kirt Manwaring. The Giants needed that big hit, and he supplied it by clearing the bases with a three-run double down the left-field line. Nomo was through.

It wasn't so much that Nomo had bad stuff that night, but more that he wasn't in command of what stuff he had. And with a division title on the line, it came at a bad time. To lighten things up a bit, the game even lost luster for some of the Japanese journalists covering Nomo. In the seventh inning and Nomo out of the game, one of the journalists fell sound asleep in a sitting position.

But neither Matt Williams nor Royce Clayton faulted Nomo. They were just happy to have a win under their belt. "He was basically the same pitcher as he was the first time we faced him in May," said Williams. "This time we got him in the stretch. He's very deceiving out of the windup, because he turns his back on you, and all of a sudden the ball's on you. When he pitches out of the stretch, he doesn't have a chance to do that.

He doesn't really have a chance to turn his back on you. So it makes it a little easier to hit the ball. He's truly unique, though, that's for sure."

Clayton, the fine young Giant shortstop, had gone four for ten against Nomo during the year. "In defense of his outing, his fastball may have lost a little bit, but he's not going to go out there and have his best stuff every night. He had arm surgery after last season. When a guy comes off surgery, he's not going to be strong the whole year. I think he's done well with the amount of innings he pitched this year. I've learned to wait on him a little more, and I think it's paid off."

Another member of the Giants liked what he saw, although he hadn't faced Nomo. Centerfielder Marvin Bernard had been called up from Phoenix (Triple A) on September 5. Bernard was born in Nicaragua and lived there until he was 12, when his family moved to Los Angeles. A lifelong Dodger fan until he was signed by the Giants, he made some interesting observations while watching Nomo from the bench.

"It seems that with his motion and the way he winds up, it looks like he is throwing hard. So you look for something that's coming in hard, and it never gets there. His motion makes you think it's going to be 95 mph. Then he throws you the forkball, and it sinks and fades away from you."

Nomo's final two starts of the 1995 season would be against the Padres, one at home and one on the road. Both were games of the utmost importance in the Dodgers' quest for the National League West title.

On September 24 against the Padres, Nomo won by a score of 6–2 but looked unimpressive. On the 30th at Jack Murphy he set the Padres down 7–2. Not only was he impressive, he clinched the National League West title for the Dodgers in the grandest fashion.

More than 50,000 fans attended Dodger Stadium for the first of the two. The Dodgers originally had considered saving Nomo for the upcoming series against the Rockies, but decided instead to pitch him against the Padres. It proved a wise move. Nomo was not at his best, but he was good enough to make it through five innings, giving up two runs on three hits. In these times, when giving up three runs in six innings is called a "quality start," Nomo's effort was adequate. What was disturbing is that he registered only two strikeouts, made 90 pitches, allowed a run to score on a wild pitch in the first inning, and flirted with five 3–2 (full) counts. He hit better than he pitched, singling in a run in the third to tie the score at 1–1.

Some say his fastball didn't register even 80 mph that night. "I can't explain it," said Mike Piazza. "He really didn't have much velocity. I think he got in a lot of deep counts and made a couple of mistakes. But Tommy had faith in the bullpen." Relievers John Commings, Antonio Osuna, Mark Guthrie, and closer Todd Worrell combined to shut out the Padres on four hits over the final four innings.

Padres coach Graig Nettles, who slugged over 300 home runs and was one of the game's top defensive third basemen during his great playing career, had mixed feelings that night and spoke candidly. "He throws a lot like Luis Tiant. He doesn't throw nearly as hard as Tiant, and he doesn't come from so many different angles as Tiant. The windup itself reminds me of Luis.

"[Tonight] he didn't have his good stuff, they tell me. I didn't come away that impressed with him by just this one outing. [But] obviously he's got good stuff, or he wouldn't have the numbers he has. The forkball looked pretty good at times. I saw him on TV earlier in the year, and it looked a lot better."

Padres third baseman Ken Caminiti had recently become the first player in history to homer from both sides of the plate three times in a season. Amazingly his switch-hitting feat came in just four games. He had never faced Nomo before. "I didn't think he was healthy," Caminiti said. "He had a good forkball, but he didn't have his fastball. He pitched two good innings, then kind of lost his good stuff. He had a good long season already. He had some arm fatigue. I heard that in the All-Star Game he had a lot better stuff."

Tony Gwynn, of course, had teamed with him in the All-Star Game and liked what he saw in Nomo, both the pitcher and the person. "When he came down to San Diego the first time this year, he came down through his interpreter and introduced himself. He said that he had seen me play and had heard of me. The guy just seems to be a level-headed guy who wants to go out there and pitch well.

"He's worked a lot this year and has thrown a lot of pitches. Facing him now, his arm looked tired. I've never seen anything like that. His delivery, I mean. It's kind of hard to figure out what you do in between the time he starts to wind up to the time he lets go. I faced him twice. I'm zero for one. I walked and lined to right. I didn't face him when he was really tough early in the year. But just watching on TV, he was very impressive."

Best stuff or not, it was an important game. By beating the Padres 6–2, Nomo upped his record to 12–6 and allowed the Dodgers to remain just a half game behind the Rockies, who beat the Giants 3–1. For the first time all season the Dodgers went 10 games over the .500 mark, with a record of 74–64. They had played good baseball, going 13–6 over the past three weeks. Now it was put up or shut up time. On the immediate horizon was a three-game series against the Rockies. So far the Dodgers had beaten the Rockies 7 out of 10. There was a matter of pressure too, or so it seemed. "Pressure!" Chad Fonville responded wryly. "No, there's no pressure at all. I can't wait for the Rockies to get here. This is the fun part."

Conventional baseball wisdom states that good pitching will beat good hitting. If this is so, then the Rockies might plead no contest. Their pitching staff, if judged by team ERA, was the worst in the National League.

On September 25, the Rockies' team ERA was an inflated 4.89. No Colorado starter, including former Cy Young winner Bret Saberhagen, had an

ERA under 4.00. By contrast, the Dodger staff had an ERA of 3.65, second only to the Braves' league-leading 3.46. Nomo and Valdes were in the National League's top five. Dodger pitchers had held opposing hitters to an average of .243, lowest in the National League, while Nomo's .181 was the best in all baseball. Opposing batters, on the other hand, had hit the Rockies pitching to the tune of a hefty .283 average. To date the entire staff had thrown only one complete game all season.

But favorable air currents or not, the Rockies could sure hit. They topped the National League in team average (.279), runs (744), total bases (2,228), triples (40), and home runs (190). Four Rockies topped the 30 mark in home runs: Dante Bichette (39), Vinnie Castilla (32), Larry Walker (32), and Andres Galarraga (30).

The Dodgers' team average was a respectable .263, with Piazza (.353, 31 HR, 91 RBI), and Karros (.296, 31 HR, 104 RBI) among the National League's top hitters, with Brett Butler leading the league with 9 triples.

"You know, I'm sick and tired of hearing the Rockies are an expansion team," Mike Piazza warned. "There's hardly an original expansion guy there. They're tough, real tough at home. We have to try to keep up with them. . . . We have a lot of young guys, a lot of guys who haven't been through this."

Piazza was right. It was foolish to think of the Rockies as an expansion club. The ownership had a hefty bankroll that had worked well on the free agent-market. Galarraga and Walker had been proven hitters before they joined the Colorado payroll. Dante Bichette had been with the Braves in 1991 and '92, while Walt Weiss, Ellis Burks, and pitchers Bill Swift and Bret Saberhagen were all seasoned vets with plenty of post-season experience among them.

It had been a strange year, to say the least. The Dodgers had not won three consecutive games since a six-game streak June 22-26. But the Rockies still had been unable to pull away in the National League West. The Dodgers had been baseball's enigma. They had been many things during the 1995 season, but the one thing they had not been was steady. "It's time to strap it on and tape it on," said Brett Butler. "People don't realize how precious this time is."

It was the biggest series of the season for the Dodgers, a three-game set against the Rockies at Dodger Stadium. Nomo and Valdes were being held back for the season-ending series against the

San Diego Padres that weekend. Against the Rockies the Dodgers would send Ramon Martinez, Tom Candiotti, and Kevin Tampani.

On September 25, a boisterous crowd of 41,984 watched as the Dodgers took over first place for the first time since September 5. Ramon Martinez lifted his record to 17–7, going eight strong innings as the Dodgers defeated the Rockies 4–3. Martinez, who had lost to the Rockies 10–1 and 9–4 in earlier back-to-back starts, threw virtually nothing but fastballs and dared them to hit it.

By winning for the 14th time in their last 20 games, the Dodgers moved a half game ahead of the Rockies with five games remaining. The two teams had not been separated by more than two games since August 5. Martinez, with help from Todd Worrell, who recorded his 31st save, shared the spotlight with Eric Karros. His two-run homer in the sixth inning off Bill Swift provided the margin of victory for the Dodgers.

The euphoria in the Dodger camp was short-lived, for the Rockies took game number two by a 7–3 score, moving back into first place. The Dodgers banged out nine hits, including two apiece by Butler, Fonville, and Mondesi, but the Dodger bullpen failed in relief of Candiotti, whose record dropped to 7–14. The Rockies' power boys could not be silenced. Just as Dante Bichette had hit his 39th homer in a losing cause off Martinez the night before, Larry Walker hit homers number 33 and 34 off Candiotti to spark the Colorado win.

The stage was set for the third and final game in this all-important series. Once again Eric Karros showed his mettle in the clutch with two hits, including his 32nd home run of the year in the seventh inning. It was Karros's 105th RBI on the year. The Dodgers were back in first, with an off day scheduled for Thursday. They received some added help from the Giants, who that day pounded the Rockies in Colorado by a 12–4 score. The Dodgers moved into San Diego's Jack Murphy Stadium on Friday, September 29, with a slim one-game lead.

With the Dodgers' 7–4 win on September 27, the tension had reached a peak. All boiled down to the three-game series with the San Diego Padres on this final weekend of the 1995 season. Valdes and Nomo had both had sufficient rest. And it was on these two young hurlers that the Dodgers would pin their title hopes.

In the first game the Dodgers sent 13-game winner Ismael Valdes against Tony Gwynn and Co. The Padres went ahead 2–0 in the fourth inning on Ken Caminiti's 26th home run of the year. The Dodgers countered with four of their own in the top of the fifth, then added another in the top of the eighth for a 5–2 lead. It seemed so close. But then the all too familiar occurred. They couldn't hold the lead. Tony Gwynn homered of Valdes in the last of the eighth to ignite a four-run Padre rally. It was the great Gwynn's third hit of the game, raising his league-leading average to .367. The Padres shut the door on the Dodgers in the ninth, and the Dodgers fell by a score of 6–5.

But the news was better out Colorado way. The Giants beat the Rockies for the second game in a row, 10–7. The Dodgers remained one game up. Did Royce Clayton and Marvin Bernard, both top schoolboy athletes in Los Angeles and admitted Dodger fans before signing with the Giants, take any special pleasure as acting as spoilers against the Rockies? The answer from both was an emphatic no. "I'm not rooting either for the Dodgers or the Rockies," said Clayton before the big series. "We're going to go out there and play the best ball we can for the five remaining games."

Bernard added a bit of humor in his thoughts. "It's funny, but when I was in L.A. I went up to Lasorda and said, 'It's a pleasure to meet you. I grew up in Los Angeles and was a big Dodger fan.' He just smiled at me and said, 'Who are you going to be cheering for?' I said I'm a Dodger fan, but I work for the Giants and I got to do my job. He just looked at me and said, 'Cheer for the Dodgers, son!' It's not being a spoiler or anything. We'll just try to do our job against the Rockies, and hopefully we can win some ball games," Bernard said before the Giants headed for Colorado. "To be honest with you, I don't care anymore about who wins the division. We can't win it, and that's what is important. Our job is to play hard and try to win as many games as we can before the season is over."

Now the pressure was on Hideo Nomo, a fitting climax to a remarkable year. The Dodgers could lock it up. Nomo held the key. If the Padres had been less than impressed with Nomo's work against them the last time around, this time they sang a different song. "He was a completely different pitcher last night," said Tony Gwynn as Nomo limited the Padres to six hits in eight innings, walking two and striking out 11 to clinch the National League West title.

With his fastball all but vanishing in recent weeks, the Dodgers were openly wondering if Nomo was hurt. He told Lasorda he was fine. He then went out to pitch the finest game he had in six weeks, beating the Padres 7–2. Nomo almost achieved one more first. A couple of more feet is all that prevented a home run. Brushed back by the Padres' Willie Blair, Nomo hit a drive that center-fielder Steve Finley chased back to the ball park's deepest point to catch.

Nomo had pitched the Dodgers to their first playoff berth since winning the 1988 World Series. The sellout crowd of 39,853 at Jack Murphy Stadium, mostly Dodger fans, it seemed, erupted in cheers the moment second baseman Delino DeShields caught the final out. Mike Piazza leaped into Todd Worrell's arms, and the celebration started. Forgetting about all the severed ligaments in his left knee, third baseman Tim Wauach leaped into the pile. Manager Tom Lasorda hugged all his coaches and put a bear hug around first baseman Eric Karros, whom he had long touted as the league's Most Valuable Player.

Such was the domino effect of Nomo's win that the Dodgers decided to start Chan Ho Park, the young Korean hurler, on the final day in Ramon Martinez's slot. Engaging in some newfound cultural know-how, Park fired a shaving cream pie into Nomo's face while the rest of the club was spraying champagne.

When the chips were down, Hideo Nomo showed the splendor from which he and his "tornado" delivery were made. He had a clear shot at Rookie of the Year honors. He finished the year with a record of 13 wins and 6 losses, a 2.54 ERA, and a league-leading 236 strikeouts. He struck out 13 or more batters in a game five times, and fanned ten or more eleven times. Sandy Koufax is the only other Dodger pitcher to strike out 10 or more in a game eight or more times. Nomo also recorded four complete games and three shutouts in the 1995 season. His three shutouts led the staff. The Dodgers were 19–9 in his 28 starts, and only 12–16 in games that immediately followed his starts.

As Frank Sinatra sang in a hit song some 30 years ago:

"It Was a Very Good Year."

# 13

# A Division Title and Broken Dreams

A full-page picture of Hideo Nomo appeared on the cover of the *Los Angeles Times Magazine* on September 17. The story, entitled "Has Nomo Saved Baseball (Well, the Dodgers Anyway)," was written by Bob Nightengale. As a baseball writer Nightengale is one of the best in the business, and he has written with more insight about Nomo than anyone in the American media. Nightengale pulls no punches in his enthusiasm for Nomo. "His first season in America went way beyond mania," Nightengale says. "The Dodger pitcher sent a jolt of energy through a sport that was on the disabled list after the strike." Sixteen photographs of Nomo in different mound and pitching positions accompanied the article. So did pictures of fans in the stands, such as one in Candlestick Park with the sign "We Hate L.A., but we love Nomo!"

Dodger attendance tells much of the story. It increased 17 percent from the first month of post-strike play to an average of 41,600 by the end of August. The Dodgers posted six sellouts in 1995, with Nomo pitching the one sellout that was not a promotional night. An average of 43,000 fans watched Nomo pitch his first ten home starts. Financially and spiritually, Nomo seemed to be just what the doctor ordered for a tainted sport.

In winning the National League West with a 78–66 record, the Dodgers were slated to battle the National League Central champion Cincinnati Reds in a five-game series, while the wild-card Colorado Rockies would lock horns with the National League East champion Atlanta Braves. The Reds were a good ball club. They closed out the year with a record of 86–59, nine games in front of runner-up Houston Astros. The last time they had reached the playoffs in 1990, they had won it all.

Cincinnati had good speed and a great defense, leading the National League in stolen bases and fielding percentage. In shortstop Barry Larkin and outfielder Reggie Sanders, the Reds had two viable MVP candidates. Sanders was among the National

League's Top Ten in ten offensive categories. Ron Gant (29 HR) and Sanders (28 HR) gave the Reds some long-ball power. The pitching staff was anchored by 18-game winner Pete Schourek (18–7), John Smiley (12–5), and Mark Portugal (11–10). By all standards the Reds were a worthy adversary.

The Dodgers' best counter was pitching. The starting trio of Hideo Nomo, Ramon Martinez, and Ismael Valdes had the potential to close off the Reds. Nomo and Valdes had ERAs at or under 3.05, and both ranked among the league leaders in strikeouts. The Dodger defense had been porous, and they had lacked steadiness throughout the year, yet it was a ball club that had shown remarkable character when things got rough.

Games one and two were to be played at Dodger Stadium, on October 3 and 4. Games three, four, and five in Cincinnati on October 6, 7, and 8.

It was a mild night at Dodger Stadium on October 3, when the Dodgers opened with 17-game winner Ramon Martinez. He had been 2–0 with a 1.93 ERA against the Reds during the regular season. The Reds had taken four out of seven against the Dodgers on the year. Martinez's mound opponent that night was Pete Schourek, whose 18 wins on the year were only one less than Greg Maddux's league-leading total of 19. Against the Dodgers Schourek had been especially tough, with a 2–0 record and a nifty 1.13 ERA.

That very morning O. J. Simpson was rendered a not-guilty verdict in the "Trial of the Century." There seemed to be a pall of sorts around Dodger Stadium, as the victory of Simpson's defense team appeared to take the life out of Dodger baseball. In the upper deck a Lance Ito lookalike appeared with five shirtless men. They all had "Guilty" written across their chest. The playoff crowd was announced at 44,199, but some present claim that there were deserted sections in the second and third decks.

Ramon Martinez, who had won six straight against the Reds, had nothing that night. He was shelled at every turn. The Reds put a four spot on the board in the first inning on a two-run double by Hal Morris and a two-run homer by Benito Santiago. By the time he left the game after 4⅓ innings, the Reds had knocked Martinez around for ten hits, two walks, and seven earned runs to take a 7–0 lead. The Dodgers scored single runs in the fifth and the sixth, scoring on a Brett Butler single and Mike Piazza's solo homer to right. The final line score for game one read: Reds, 7 runs on 12 hits, Dodgers, 2 runs on 8 hits. "Everybody's saying it was a weird day in the city, but we came out ready," insisted Brett Butler. "Sometimes you just get a performance that shuts you down. The character on this club was built on adversity. We'll see what happens tomorrow night."

The next night was no better. The game was closer, but the Dodgers literally threw it away. The pitching matchup pitted Ismael Valdes against the Reds' John Smiley. A disappointing crowd of 46,051, well short of capacity, watched as the Reds downed the Dodgers 5–4 to put Los Angeles two games down. Poor fielding and lack of clutch hitting all but obviated the heroics of Eric Karros. He drove in all four Dodger runs, on a double in the first inning and homers in the fourth and ninth, the latter a two-run shot.

But the Dodgers stranded 11 runners on the bases, eight of them in the fifth, sixth, and seventh innings. "You can't give away runs," a frustrated Karros said. "You can't get 14 hits but leave 11 men on. The way we played, we didn't deserve to win."

The temperature was in the fifties and the crowd numbered 53,276 at Cincinnati's Riverfront Stadium the night of October 6. The pre-game analysis by Jim Palmer and company introduced some food for thought. Mike Piazza had stranded seven runners Tuesday night, but that was not the major concern. "He's going to hit forever," said Palmer. The more important question was how Hideo Nomo and Mike Piazza would handle the running game of the Cincinnati Reds. Why would this be more difficult for Nomo and Piazza? The reason, Palmer stated, was that Nomo threw a split-finger fastball, and that's the most difficult pitch to throw a runner out on if you're a catcher. Because the Reds were a team that could beat you so many ways, "the best thing Nomo can do," said Palmer, "is to throw a no-hitter."

Despite a record of 13–16 in September, it is wrong to minimize the efficiency of the Reds ball club. As Jim Palmer noted, the Reds play the game in "fast forward." In the National League they were first in stolen bases, second in runs, and third in home runs. Defensively there was no better team in the league. They made only 79 errors all year. "If the right guys get on for the Reds tonight," he went on to say, "Mike Piazza's going to think he's at a track meet."

The Dodgers were in big trouble, down 2 games to 0 in the series. It had come down to one game. What might be left to the 1995 season rested largely in Nomo's hands. Fourteen years earlier Fernando Valenzuela had taken the mound with the Dodgers in a similar position. He won Game 4 of the division series against the Houston Astros. He won Game 5 of the best of five National League Championship Series against the Montreal Expos. And with the Dodgers down by a two-game deficit in the 1981 World Series against the Yankees, he pitched a complete-game victory in Game 3. The Dodgers went on to win four straight and capture the World Series title.

Nomo had never pitched in a post-season game in Japan. No matter what happened tonight, however, would not blight a season he would always cherish. When he signed with the Dodgers in January, his only request had been that he be given an opportunity to win a starting job in the rotation. Fred Claire obliged by promising he would not sign a free-agent starter.

Since the All-Star Game, Nomo's record had been 7–5 with a 3.03 ERA. It was not as impressive as his first-half statistics, to be sure, but good pitching nonetheless. He was tough when they needed him, winning the biggest game of the season against the San Diego Padres. "Throughout the season," Nomo said before the game, "I've always wanted to do my best. I still do."

It was not to be. Although that "no-hitter" comment by Jim Palmer was said in a bit of jest, there was also an element of foreboding. That night the

Dodgers remained even more frigid, while the Reds could not be cooled off. Nomo's big game against San Diego had helped dispel speculation that he was hurt. But his fastball was still clocked down the stretch as between 75–80 mph–ten mph slower than usual. And against the Reds in Game 3 he had little left. The Reds jumped all over him for seven hits and five runs on the way to a 10–1 win, and swept the Dodgers out of the series.

Nomo's mound opponent in Game 3 was southpaw David Wells, the third straight left-hander the Reds sent against the Dodgers in the series. Known as a flake around the baseball circuit, Wells had previously appeared in nine post-season games for the Toronto Blue Jays. In an interesting footnote, the Dodgers had not had a left-handed starting pitcher since Bobby Ojeda started a game for them in 1992.

To those who remembered Nomo's one-hitter in Candlestick Park in August, it was clear from the start that he was not nearly as sharp tonight. The splitter was not splitting as much, and his velocity was wanting. Moreover, as Palmer had warned, the Reds were running on him, stealing three bases in the first two innings.

In the bottom of the third Barry Larkin singled off Nomo with one out. Up to the plate came Ron

Gant. Nomo delivered a fastball, and Gant sent it flying deep into the left field bleachers for a home run, putting Cincinnati ahead 2–0. Gant, who had been on a 1 for 19 dry spell, hadn't homered since September 4, a stretch of 64 at-bats.

The Dodgers closed the gap to 2–1 when, in the top of the fourth, Raul Mondesi looped a single to center to score Eric Karros, who was on second as the result of a two-base error by Reggie Sanders.

The Reds made it 3–1 in the bottom of the fourth on a solo home run by Bret Boone over the wall in center. Boone, the son of Kansas City manager Bob Boone and grandson of former American League RBI champ Ray Boone, has often said that he lives for high fastballs. That's just what he got from Nomo, and he hammered it out of sight.

Nomo set the Dodgers down in the fifth, but by the sixth inning he was spent. A sign in the Cincinnati bleachers read, "NO MO LOS ANGELES." It was not long either. After allowing two hits in the top of the fifth, Nomo was through. His season was over. Kevin Tapani was called in and walked Boone to fill the bases. Lasorda immediately replaced him with Mark Guthrie. Reds manager Davey Johnson countered by having Mark Lewis pinch-hit for Branson. Lewis responded well, hitting the first pinch-hit grand slam home run in playoff history, and the first of his career, to put the Reds ahead 7–1. The Reds scored three more times in the bottom of the seventh, and the series was history.

It was only the second time the Dodgers had been swept in 27 post-season series since 1916, and Reds skipper Davey Johnson had a hand in both. He was also the second baseman for the Orioles when Baltimore blanked the Dodgers in the 1966 World Series. "I've seen a lot of playoffs, and this was the most devastating," said Tommy Lasorda, whose contract had yet to be renewed for 1996. In the three-game series the Dodgers were outscored 22–7.

It was a disappointing ending. "I don't think we got a key hit in the whole series," said Eric Karros. "We probably played our worst offensive baseball of the year. For lack of a better phrase, Cincinnati flat-out kicked our butts." Karros was on target. The Dodgers had left 30 men on base. Their average with runners in scoring position was an anemic .167. Tim Wallach, who had waited 14 years for a playoff chance was 1 for 12 (0.83). Mike Piazza, their heaviest hitter, and league runner-up in batting, was 3 for 14 (.214). The much heralded Raul Mondesi went 2 for 10 (.200).

When Hideo Nomo departed the game in the sixth inning, Jim Palmer said it perfectly: "Brilliant year, this game notwithstanding for Hideo Nomo, who really captured everybody's fancy." After the game Nomo, who gives only brief answers to reporters' questions, said only that he didn't pitch that badly. "They hit my good fastball," he said. Certainly even with a faded fastball, his six strikeouts in five innings still say something.

He had a wonderful season. Even a tired arm and a split fingernail on his pitching hand toward the end did not diminish praise from San Francisco Giant batting coach Bobby Bonds. "Nomo's deceptive, he's substance," Bonds said. "Great location with the fastball, and an unhittable forkball because you can't pick it up." Long-time baseball scouts will tell you that his forkball is among the best they have ever seen. Hitters will say that it is impossible to distinguish between his forkball and fastball, which often finds them swinging at balls in the dirt.

Yet despite the fastballs and forkballs, despite the mega strikeouts and the sand and the sea of southern California, it had not been an easy journey. Those who reach the top will tell you that celebrity status has a price. And Los Angeles has always been the city of celebrities. When Nomo's pitching went flat in late August, Lasorda blamed in part these many distractions.

"I still have trouble getting used to all this attention," Nomo said. "Everybody wants my autograph. In Japan it's not like that. They just want to know the person. Then they can go and tell their friends. Here everybody wants me to sign. Maybe it's because I sign in Japanese. I don't know if I'll ever get used to all the autographs."

As Hideo Nomo readied himself to return to his home in Osaka, Japan, where he has become his country's reigning hero, there was still an aura of wonderment. As he recalled the trepidation he experienced eight months earlier, not in his wildest thoughts had he envisioned fitting so snugly into the culture this soon, in his first season with the Los Angeles Dodgers. He could call the local pizza place near his West Los Angeles home and have them ask if he wanted "the usual." Or take a walk along the Venice Beach boardwalk with his wife, Kikuko, and three-year-old son, Takhiro, as just another family strolling along on a sunny day.

Nomo finished his rookie season with a record of 13 wins and 6 losses, a winning percentage of 6.84. His earned run average of 2.54 was second only to Greg Maddux's brilliant 1.63. Moreover, of all the National League starting pitchers, only Maddux, Nomo, and the San Diego Padres' Andy Ashby (2.94) had an ERA under 3.00. Nomo's 1.73 ERA at home was the best in the National League. He struck out a league high 236 batters, allowing but 124 hits in 191.1 innings or just 5.83 hits per nine innings pitched, the best in the National League. His average strikeout rate of 11.10 per nine innings was also by far the league's best. Among all National League pitchers, only the Braves' Greg Maddux could boast a better 1995.

"I don't think any of us ever expected anything like this," said Nomo's agent, Don Nomura. "Now I've got my phone ringing off the hook with endorsements, advertisers, people wanting to do movies, write books, everything." And one thing is especially certain. Because of Hideo Nomo, baseball will never be the same either in Japan or in the United States.

# 14

# A Hero Returns

**H**e came back a conquering hero. Hideo Nomo was greeted by a crowd of screaming, camera-wielding fans when he returned to Japan on October 16. More than 500 fans and reporters packed two levels in the waiting area at Tokyo's Narita Airport, pressing against police ropes. Some cameramen and photographers knocked one another over in the crush as Nomo walked through. At an airport hotel shortly after his arrival, he held a news conference. He talked about the season, a bit about the Dodgers and a desire just to be left alone for a while. "I just want to relax," he said.

Nomo made it clear that he needed some good solid rest and recuperation. "He let everyone know that his television appearances were going to be few and far between, according to Mitsufumi Okabe, who heads the Japan Television Network in San Francisco. "The only official event he will be participating in is the wedding of his closest friend, a star baseball player in Japan. Otherwise he plans to stay home with his family and begin his training for next year."

In an era when athletes and entertainers have lots of things to say about almost everything, including things they know nothing about, Nomo resents the media's intrusion into his personal life. At all costs he protects his family and keeps them as far away as possible from the public eye. Conspicuously, during his news conferences and limited TV appearances, his family is never with him.

"They showed only him and nothing of his family. That's Nomo's policy," says Akira Matsuo of the Mainichi Newspapers, who spent two weeks in Japan following Nomo's return. "There was never much press about his background or his young days. I'm not sure whether that is intentional or not."

What he did say was how much he enjoyed playing baseball in the United States, and how much the season meant to him. That he was so happy for the opportunity to live out a dream. According to Mitsufumi Okabe, Nomo has also indicated a strong interest in having a place on next year's Olympic committee for the Japanese team that will represent his country at the 1996 Summer Olympic Games in Atlanta.

He had a number of good things to say about his Los Angeles Dodger teammates. He specified catcher Mike Piazza in particular for being a good teacher who helped him learn about the National League hitters. Those who watched Nomo pitch all season noticed that he rarely if ever shook off a sign from Piazza.

For his part, Piazza has said how much it bugs him when reporters ask questions that he considers "ridiculous" at best and a lot of "crap" at worst. "One day [Nomo] gave me this entire video machine setup just for putting up with all of this crap, I think," Piazza says. One of the favorite questions, which sprung up in every city, according to Piazza, was how he communicated with Nomo. "That's never been a problem," Piazza attests. "He knows more than he's letting on, believe me.

"In the beginning, I learned three words in Japanese. *Ogenki desuka*, which means, 'How ya doin'? *Shuchu*, which means concentrate. And when, say, there are runners on first and second and one out, I holler at him, 'Double play!' "

Piazza always felt that things would be better if everybody just left Nomo alone. "It's ridiculous. You come into the clubhouse and everyone's waiting for him."

Nomo also told people that he began to feel more and more a part of the team as the season wore on. On the other hand, Nomo's teammates treated him like they would any other rookie, which included a few pranks. One night the players got together and stole his clothes, leaving in their place clothes from the disco era. They stood around waiting for Nomo's reaction, not sure if he had understood what happened. But he laughed and shook his head. He caught on, all right, and went along with the joke. "I thought it was funny," Nomo said. "Not that I want them to do it a lot, but since I'm still a rookie, it was okay."

Although his interpreter, Michael Okumura, was constantly at his side in the clubhouse, in time Nomo gained enough confidence to venture alone to certain restaurants. "It became a lot easier for me. At first most Americans looked the same to me, all Americans looked alike, sort of how Americans think Japanese people look alike. Now I can tell the difference."

More perhaps than all the accolades, Nomo indicated how thrilled he had been to have pitched for a team that won something. Although he had lost the game in Cincinnati, his great thrill was in clinching the National League West title. It was a feeling that he had never experienced before. Surprisingly, Nomo had never been on a ball club that had won a title of any kind. Not with the Buffaloes, not in high school, not even in junior high. He simply won't let the media get too close to him. They want him to give interesting insightful answers to a multitude of questions. They want to know what he really thinks and feels. But Nomo refuses to bare his soul.

If Nomo's public appearances in Japan have been limited, his commercials are everywhere. "I watched TV during my recent two weeks in Japan," Akira Matsuo says, "and the commercials are all over. Some are with Tommy Lasorda. He even seems to smile more now. He seems more Americanized. He seems very happy." When asked how he compared Japanese baseball with American baseball, he wisely avoided controversy. He said only that there was a big difference, but the way to find out is to play ball in the United States.

There was lots to be happy about. In September Nomo had been chosen Japan's top sports hero for 1995. He ranked first among all outstanding sports figures in the eyes of many Japanese fathers and boys. He was followed closely by Ichiro Suzuki, the batting leader of the Pacific League's pennant-winning Orix Blue Wave. The survey questioned 300 fathers and as many high school and elementary school boys. It was conducted in mid-September before Athletics Day, a national holiday that commemorates the 1964 Tokyo Olympic Games.

Interestingly, the poll showed that 36.3 percent of the respondents said they wanted their children to become outstanding athletes. Nomo and Suzuki were followed by pro soccer player Kazuyoshi Miura, Shiego Nagashima, former pro baseball star and now manager of the Central League's Yomiuri Giants, and Kimiko Date, Japan's ace female tennis player.

One of the lingering questions is how Nomo's success will affect the baseball scene in Japan. Most significant, of course, is that for 30 years the Japanese didn't really know how their players compared to America's. There is also good indication that with the expanded major league market, and a general consensus that there is a depleted talent pool here in the United States, that the line between baseball in Japan and baseball here is becoming thinner. Also, as people like Masanori Murakami and Matt Williams say, the aggressive nature of many American ballplayers is a delight for a pitcher like Nomo.

"They play a power game here," says Murakami, "and you're going to be hurt by the home run now and then. But not as often by the single or the double. In Japan the style of the game is different. If you throw ball four—or even ball one or ball two—they will not swing at it. They swing only at strikes. Here they try to hit everything out. They do not require the ball to be a strike."

His assessment is well taken. Crafty pitchers, including many old-timers like Larry Jansen, who pitched the New York Giants to a National League flag in 1951, then coached the likes of Juan Marichal, Gaylord Perry, and Fergie Jenkins in the 1960s and early '70s, insist they'd love to pitch to these big free swingers. "I think the scouts are making a big mistake today," says Jansen, who won 96 games for the New York Giants between 1947 and 1951. "They are signing players who can throw hard, and they don't seem to care if they can't hit the wall. I probably wouldn't have got a chance to play professional ball under those conditions."

Nomo, like Greg Maddux, pitches with his head as well as his arm. According to reports, so do many other top Japanese pitchers. The message is clear: pitchers who think rather than just throw hard will do well against free-swinging American batters.

It is clear to people like Akira Matsuo and Mitsufumi Okabe, who travel regularly between Japan and the United States, that high school baseball players are starting to set their sights westward now that Nomo has done so well. "Papers are mentioning all the time just who might be the next Nomo," says Matsuo. Certainly he has given young boys an American dream, as more and more of them can watch Nomo on TV.

Almost any top-quality Japanese player will be welcome with open arms in the United States after seeing the amount of money Nomo has generated for the Dodgers. West Coast teams are becoming especially interested in Japanese players. According to sources close to the scene in Japan, there are three Japanese pitchers right now who are considered good enough to pitch in the major leagues. Others like Bobby Valentine say the number may be as high as twenty. There are at least six pitchers who are contemplating leaving Japan for the United States. As we have seen, Japanese players must wait ten years to declare free agency. But they could simply retire as Nomo did, and make themselves available to the American market. During Japan's own All-Star Game the 12 team owners had a special meeting. Understandably, they were nervous. While they applaud Nomo's success, they still don't want to see others jump ship.

Wherever Nomo pitched—New York, San Francisco, Chicago, St. Louis, Houston, Philadelphia, Pittsburgh—Japanese American fans flocked to see him. In San Francisco there is good indication that Japan Day will become a yearly event with the Giants.

Jim Lefebvre, who was the Oakland A's hitting instructor and played and coached for five years in Japan, thinks that Nomo's move will make others want to follow him. "The great players want to play in the best league. It's going to be like it was in the Negro Leagues after the majors finally opened the door for Jackie Robinson."

Lefebvre might be stretching things a bit. Valentine, who was fired by the Chiba Lotte Marines after the season, thinks a run on the major leagues is unlikely. "The players here make good money, they can play until they drop, they have potential jobs for life, and they know the language, food and travel. . . . I don't know how many other Japanese players have the same desire to delve into the unknown."

Nomo's agent, Don Nomura, agrees with Valentine that most players would consider it too big a risk. It's difficult to throw everything away and to start a new life, Nomura believes. "I think Nomo made a real history making move, but the real measure of it is that it should enhance the position of Japanese players, who have been restricted by a system similar to the communist party, with no reserve rules, no free agency, no real voice in negotiations. They have been like puppets on a string to the corporations owning the teams. Whether they follow Nomo or use it as leverage, they are now in a position to make a better deal."

In fact, Nomura has attempted to institute a player-management system in Japan as Marvin Miller did in America, but has not exactly been received with open arms by the owners. "I think Japanese baseball is afraid to open their markets. . . . They're putting a lock on the door."

So whether there will be a rush on Japanese players coming to America is still a question. Nomo got here in the first place with a loophole in the rules. The rest, of course, is history, and whether this is the exception rather than an impending norm is still uncertain.

One thing that will be on Nomo's mind is negotiating next year's contract. He plans to make several trips to the United States before the start of the 1996 season, but has yet to mention anything specifically about a new contract. The attitudes of many young Japanese are changing, and Nomo has impacted this change accordingly. His ideas are independent, and he doesn't necessarily go along with the desires of his coaches and manager in Japan. People close to Japanese baseball believe that the manager and coaches of the Dodgers gave him more freedom and less constraints, especially in allowing himself to train as he sees fit. It seems likely that Nomo will be playing baseball in the United States until he retires. He has given no indication that he will return to play professional baseball in Japan.

On October 8, Tommy Lasorda was signed to a one-year contract with the Dodgers, returning for his 20th year. And there have been some changes: Jose Offerman and Tim Wallach are gone from the left side of the infield. Free agent Greg Gagne signed for a one-year $2.6 million deal, and will replace Offerman at short. Within the same 24-hour period the Dodgers landed third baseman Mike Blowers (.257, 23 HR, 96 RBI) in a trade with the Seattle Mariners. The Dodgers re-signed right-hander Ramon Martinez to a four-year $15 million contract and reliever Todd Worrell to a one-year $4 million contract with an option for 1997. The Dodgers also re-signed Brett Butler for 1996 and have also re-signed second baseman Delino De-Shields.

The bucks are there for Nomo. The Dodgers are expected to offer him about $500,000 for the 1996 season, $65,000 more than they paid right-fielder Raul Mondesi after he was named Rookie of the Year. Nomo's attorneys, believing he is a special case, will probably shoot for something in excess of $1 million. Invariably there will be an incentive bonus based on attendance as well. What makes the Dodgers' starting rotation so interesting is that all four starters for next year will be foreign born, as Chan Ho Park, a South Korean, is slated to replace Tom Candiotti in the rotation.

As for Nomo, all indication is that he will get every bit of what he asks for. When the Dodgers offered Nomo a rookie salary of $109,000 and a million-dollar bonus, Nomura told them it wasn't enough and made plans to continue on to New York. So O'Malley found another million, and Hideo Nomo became a Los Angeles Dodger.

# Rookie of the Year

It had been a wonderful year for Nomo, a fulfillment of a dream. He had come to the United States to take on the best in the world. He became a Los Angeles Dodger and a strikeout king. He started the 1995 All-Star Game and won the game that clinched National League West for the Dodgers. He was Hideo Nomo, and his name alone radiated a new and exciting mania through two countries.

Through the blazing months of June and July there seemed to be little doubt that Nomo had a lock on Rookie of the Year honors. In the month of June he had been devastating to opposing batters. But with the dog days of August and the uncertainty of September, Nomo's lock on Rookie of the Year was no longer certain. The Braves' Chipper

Jones seemed to be gaining ground, and in some circles had even passed Nomo.

In its final Power Report rankings *USA Today Baseball Weekly* announced Jones as its top rookie. The Atlanta third baseman barely nosed out Nomo by two votes, 24 to 22, while the two split the first-place ballots 3 to 3. *Baseball Weekly* argued that Jones, a season removed from a severe leg injury, "anchored the hot corner, while joining Fred McGriff, David Justice, and Ryan Klesko as home run and RBI muscle on the team." Without negating a thing from Nomo's résumé, they mentioned only that the Dodger pitcher was hurt by the perception that his five years' playing in Japan gave him veteran experience.

Jones had played solid baseball for the Braves, who were heading for their first World Series title since 1957, when the franchise resided in Milwaukee. He put some nice numbers on the board (.265, 23 HR, 86 RBI). Writers such as Dave Kindred of the *Sporting News*, and Peter Pascarelli of *Baseball Weekly* opted for Jones. "My vote goes to Jones, who had a better year than Nomo, who faded down the stretch," Pascarelli wrote in his Major League Report for *Baseball Weekly* on November 8. "And when in doubt, vote for an everyday player over a starting pitcher."

In touting Jones—who made 25 errors at third base—over Nomo, Kindred applauded Jones's gritty determination and ability, and the fact that he has that intangible quality which conveys stardom, that same quality that characterized Mickey Mantle and Eddie Mathews in their rookie years in the early 1950s. Certainly both the Mick and Eddie Mathews went on to baseball greatness and worthy Hall of Fame careers, but neither of these two baseball greats won Rookie of the Year.

Nomo, of course, had many boosters and advocates, none more determined than Bob Nightengale of the *Los Angeles Times*, who covered Nomo's entire season. Nomo, he felt, "not only saved the Dodgers, but perhaps all of baseball" in 1995. But this fact alone should not obscure Nomo's sensational feats on the diamond, which made him a deserving Rookie of the Year. Nightengale made many cogent points to support his claim: Nomo's 16 strikeouts on June 14 established a Dodger rookie record. His 236 strikeouts on the year broke the previous Dodger rookie record of 209 set by Don Sutton in 1965. Nomo struck out 13 or more batters in a game 5 different times, and he fanned 10 or more 11 different times.

He was the National League's starting pitcher and pitched two scoreless innings in the All-Star

Game, the first rookie to start an All-Star Game since Fernando Valenzuela in 1981. He clinched the National League West title for the Dodgers on September 30, striking out 11 and allowing just one earned run in a 7–2 win over the San Diego Padres. He pitched a one-hitter and fanned 11 at San Francisco on August 5. He won seven decisions in a row between June 2 and July 15. Included are six straight wins in June with an 0.89 ERA. He was the National League Player of the Month for June. He led the league in strikeouts and held opposing batters to less hits per nine innings than any other pitcher in the National League.

His very name started a new "mania" in baseball that spread across two continents. The Dodgers were 19–9 in the 28 games he started. He recorded four complete games, and his three shutouts led the Dodger staff. His earned run average of 2.54 was the second lowest in the National League. All this from a rookie right-hander from Japan, whose big goal six months earlier was just to win a starting job in the Dodger rotation.

The season ended with the Atlanta Braves defeating the Cincinnati Reds in the National League Championship Series, then going on to defeat the Cleveland Indians in the World Series. Playing for the world champions could not help but add a little luster to Chipper Jones's candidacy for Rookie of the Year. But it would be nearly another month until the final voting was announced.

Tony Woods, who spent seven years with the Chicago Cub organization in the 1980s, extended his kudos to Nomo and strongly touts Nomo as Rookie of the Year. "Chipper Jones had a great season," Woods pointed out. "But then he got to sit in the lap of luxury. When you have guys like David Justice and Fred McGriff hitting behind you, you get good pitches to hit. You're sitting in the prime of the lineup in the third position, and that's the best position to get good pitches."

As Woods emphasized, the Braves would still have been winners without Jones in the lineup. With all their talent, they would have probably reached the top anyway. On the other hand, Nomo carried the Dodgers through a losing first half of the season. It could well be argued that without Nomo, the Dodgers would not have won their division, or for that matter even a wild-card slot.

The experts and pundits may have straddled the fence between Jones and Nomo. But on November 8 the Baseball Writers of America gave Rookie of the Year honors to Hideo Nomo. He received 18 first-place votes and finished with 118 points in balloting by the 28-member committee, which consists of two writers in each big league city.

Jones, who helped the Braves run away with the National League East and go on to win the World Series, received 10 first-place votes and finished with 104 points. Second baseman Quilvio Veras of the Florida Marlins finished a distant third with 14 votes, and New York Mets pitcher Jason Isringhausen finished fourth with 4 votes.

This marked the fourth straight year that a Dodger player has been named Rookie of the Year, and the second time the club has dominated the award over a four-year stretch of time. It was Eric Karros, Mike Piazza, Raul Mondesi and Hideo Nomo in 1992, '93, '94 and '95. From 1979 through 1982, it was Rick Sutcliffe, Steve Howe, Fernando Valenzuela, and Steve Sax.

Moreover, it marked the 15th time that a Brooklyn or a Los Angeles Dodger first-year player captured the award since Jackie Robinson had become the first recipient in 1947, giving the Dodgers more than twice as many of the awards as any other team. In the National League the Reds are a distant second with six Rookies of the Year. In the American League, the Yankees, and the Orioles (once the St. Louis Browns) have each had seven rookies of the year each.

It was a grand moment for Nomo. "I'm very, very proud of what he's done," said Tommy Lasorda, "and I expect him to do better next year than he did this year." Nomo was also very pleased, and allowed for no ambiguity as to what he hoped for next year. "For next season I'd like to target the World Series," Nomo said from Japan through a translator during a conference call.

No less than an authority than pitching great Nolan Ryan has also been impressed by the Hideo Nomo happening. Just as Ryan did over his brilliant 27-year career, in 1995 Nomo made things happen. Just to know he was pitching on a given day captured the baseball fancy of all concerned. There was always the possibility of something great happening. Always the possibility that he would show you something different.

"Let's put it this way," Nolan Ryan said before the All-Star Game. "If I wasn't involved in baseball at all, I'd still be watching this game. "Baseball needs events like Nomo."

And it's a story that's far from over.